Dear
you

TESSA BROAD

Dear you

A Letter to my unborn children

RedDoor

Published by RedDoor
www.reddoorpublishing.com

ISBN 978-1-910453-40-7

A CIP catalogue record for this book is available from the
British Library

Cover design: Clare Connie Shepherd
www.paintedbyclare.co.uk

Typesetting: Tutis Innovative E-Solutions Pte. Ltd

Printed and bound by Nørhaven, Denmark

For my mum and in loving memory of my dad

Why write a letter you will never send?
Why express your love for people who never existed?
Why not?

Dear You

I'm not sure how many people I'm writing to here. Sometimes I've imagined myself with two children, sometimes with three. It doesn't matter how many I've imagined, none of you came into being so why am I writing to you? For catharsis? For closure? Lordy as I write the word 'closure' I'm hearing it said in an American accent for it sounds so self-helpy/psychobabble, but no, 'closure' is not the reason; nor catharsis. I'm writing to you simply because I feel that I know you, that I love you; and I'd like you to get to know me. I want this letter to feel like you have spent time with me and me with you.

If children had happened for me when I wanted them to, you would by now be grown-ups. So I will write to you as your adult selves and tell you about the mother I would have been to you and the childhood I envisaged for you. I will pass on the family rituals that I would have invented for my real children. I'll talk to you of my values, my loves and my pet hates. I'll write about the big stuff, like coping with the loss of a loved one; the importance of kindness; and why I think it's vital to follow your hearts and dreams in order to craft a life that you love. I will also tell you how to make tasty lump-free gravy; how to make your home smell like it's been cleaned from top to bottom just from hoovering the hall; what to say in a condolence card; and I'll let you in on a unique way to stop an insect bite from itching. I'll also tell you how I longed to hear you call me Mummy.

As we are never to meet, I can be your perfect mother. My dreams of motherhood can remain a rosy-coloured vision for me and you, my imagined children, can be all I would have wanted you to be and that is not to be perfect, but to be perfectly yourselves.

Having said that, now that you are adults you are rarely in my thoughts. I no longer need you there. This would, obviously, be an unspeakably cruel thing to say to a real child, but not for one that's invented. It's like the imaginary friend of the lonely or creative youngster. When that 'friend' is no longer required it feels like a positive thing, a sign of healing perhaps. Indeed, the fact I no longer need you is freeing for me. It means I have reached a place of peace where I am no longer struggling to play a role I wasn't cast for. This letter is an indulgence for me at a time when the children of my friends and family are, like you, becoming adults and so for my contemporaries the role of grandparent might soon be beckoning. It's another job I will be unqualified to do, but it's a situation that this time around I won't need to imagine.

I will recount the journey I took to try to bring you into my life. How the quest to conceive you made me feel. What I lost and gained along the way and how the woebegone, wannabe mummy that I once was became the woman I am now: childless but chilled, sailing through Mother's Day with a smile on my face. I will be honest with you and at times my language will be candid and the subject explicit, but I hope most of all to make you smile.

I feel I must be writing this letter to a daughter and I would have named you Lily after my maternal grandmother, a woman I have never met, as she died aged forty-one when my own mother was just fifteen. While I never knew my grandma I have always felt a strong connection to her.

As a child I was always drawn to children who had lost a parent, luckily they were few in number but I felt my mother's loss keenly. I can pinpoint the moment when I first felt her grief and sadness. I would have been aged around five and it was at the funeral of my paternal grandfather. We were at the house of one of my aunties, at a window looking out at the hearse and funeral cars. I was standing in front of my mother, leaning back into the comfort of her body, her hands were on my shoulders and I heard her say: 'I'd give anything to see my mum again.' I think I knew she was just saying it to herself but I chirped in, 'Would you give me?' She didn't answer. The grown-up me knows that funerals often result in a revisiting of grief and loss from the past but I can remember that little girl feeling a twinge of disappointment when the resounding 'NO!' wasn't forthcoming.

Sensing that profound loss so young I believe has shaped me and that it might be part of why (deeply buried in my subconscious) I didn't become your mother, for fear that I too might have to leave you one day and cause you the same pain. Of course, I'm not a psychoanalyst and it could simply have been because my ovaries weren't fit for purpose.

I have been told that Lily senior was a wonderful lady; that she was a wise, loving, kind and affectionate woman and that she was most particularly non-judgemental. It's a core belief of mine, the old Native American proverb 'Do not judge your neighbour until you walk two moons in their moccasins.' I sometimes stray from it and have to remind myself not to judge, but I know I would have tried to pass this way of living down to you. When I hit my forties, my mum told me that I reminded her of her mother, in both looks and disposition; it felt like a gift.

In my imaginings I would be writing to at least one son, maybe two. I'm not sure what names I would have given you. Perhaps my husband and I might have chosen to go down the Victoria and David Beckham route and name our children from the place name of his or her conception. Any of you children might have been called Portland, Cromwell, Central Middlesex or University College Hospital for reasons that will become clear later. I suppose I could also have chosen a quirky 'Test tube' for you to suffer all your days.

Whatever your names, when you were babies I would imagine holding your squashy little bodies, breathing in your scent, feeling your oh so soft skin against mine. I'd gaze in wonder at your tiny hands, toes and noses. I'd imagine your giggles and gurgles and the dinky little clothes I'd have dressed you in. Conversely, I know I would have baulked at the ghastly, primary-coloured plastic toys I'd have had to acquire. I would have let you have them but all the while I would have been craving something antique or vintage looking, made of wood or metal and stored neatly in an aesthetically pleasing toy box.

I wouldn't have been averse to a bit of mess though. I enjoy my orderly, clutter-free, clean home of the childless but I would have enthusiastically dived into the carnage that goes with potato printing, papier mâché and the like. We would have baked together too and whenever I bake every work surface in the kitchen is covered in debris: flour, eggshells, sugar, and all manner of spillages, so adding small children to the mix wouldn't greatly have increased the mess I already create all by myself. I am also inclined to narrate out loud a *Great British Bake Off*-style commentary to amuse myself while I bake.

We might also have been little 'sewing bees' and I would have told you of the calamity that accompanied my first sewing project. I arrived home from school triumphant clutching my homemade pencil case (with fitted zip) but I felt it looked a little creased and so, spotting the ironing board out with a still warm iron atop it, I gave it a quick press before showing it to my mum. Sadly I wasn't to know that the material issued by the school was of a synthetic nature, which meant my carefully crafted pencil case ended up a shrivelled, molten mess stuck to the iron. It didn't put me off needlework; just ironing, which wasn't difficult.

I've often imagined entertaining ourselves; say on a wet afternoon, February half-term maybe, by holding a mini disco in our kitchen. Kitchen discos in my opinion can be enjoyed at any age. The music is always great and you can be the star of the dance floor. Dancing seems to be prohibited when you reach a certain age, which I think is a shame. For sure I would have embarrassed you beyond belief at any event attended by the whole family that included alcohol and a dance floor. I love a bop and with a few drinks aboard I think I am Beyoncé and/or Madonna (I'm rather too fond of saying that she's older than me) but I imagine it is true even for her; yes, for sure the sexy dance-floor gyrations of Madonna's 'trying too hard days' would have embarrassed the hell out of her adolescent daughter.

I've pictured us watching football matches together, both at home, on TV, and gloriously live at Wembley and Portman Road. World Cups, Champions League and Ipswich Town[1], yeah OK it's not like watching Brazil, though actually in view of their 2014 World Cup performance, it is! I've imagined teaching you how to swim and that would have to be in the sea, as that was where I was taught, so much better spitting out salty seaweedy water than the chlorinated stuff I think.

---

[1] Truth be told you would, I'm sure, have become Manchester City supporters (your 'father's' team), which would be a pleasure now, but in the days of your early childhood, something to be endured.

I have envisaged these moments and many more like them hundreds of times; the little things of parenthood, like seeing you running towards me and feeling your little arms wrapping around my legs. Your delighted faces as the first cake you cook comes out of the oven and when your first piece of artwork is magnetically attached to the fridge in our kitchen. The thrill of feeling the line go tight when catching your first fish, the joy when the stabilisers come off your bikes (do they still do stabilisers?)…the list is long. Needless to say I have spent less time imagining the toddler tantrums, the school-age stand-offs…and the teenage tensions.

I'm not sure I felt it when I was of childbearing age, but I fear I might have had a yearning around the time you reached school age to reinvent myself as something of a 'yummy' in the 'mummy' department, progressing hopefully, to a MILF as you and I got older (ha?!). I am ever so slightly vain I suppose, though mostly I think it is actually a lack of self-confidence that makes me place such an importance on my appearance. A flaw in my character I would hope not to pass on. However, I do hold with the idea that if you look good, you feel good and you'll learn later that I think feeling good is something of a priority in this life. I also believe that a concern for your appearance is simply a way of taking care of yourself and what could be more worthy than that? Thinking about it though; I imagine my morning beauty routines and careful outfit selection may well have been abandoned had I become an actual mother because of the sheer exhaustion and lack of time. However, I cannot picture myself at the school gate without mascara whatever the level of fatigue; my eyelashes, while long, have fair ends you see. Luckily for me though, my hair would need little attention. I have owned the 'Bedhead' look for years. I wonder if any of you would have inherited my tangled, curly mess of a hairstyle.

So, when did you first appear in my imagination? By the way, I should tell you, I do have a vivid imagination and spend my days visualising all sorts of strange and wonderful things.

'You may say I'm a dreamer, but I'm not the only one.'

I have an elephantine memory for events and moments in my life and while I know I will be one among many, I remember exactly where I was the day the man who wrote those words died. I was a student in Sheffield and I got a lift to lectures every Monday, from a guy whose name I can't remember, but we were on the same Business Studies course. That morning, 8 December 1980, while I was waiting for whatshisname to pick me up, I heard on the radio that John Lennon had been shot dead.

'If you have a great passion it seems that the logical thing is to see the fruit of it, and the fruit are children.' Roman Polanski

I like this quote, but Lordy, it's a tad inappropriate since the author of it, Polanski, had sex with a thirteen-year-old girl. I'm not sure how we apply the core belief of not judging here either. Anyway at the age of around twenty-eight I decided I'd like to see the 'fruit of my passion' and started 'trying for a family'. Quietly and slowly the images of you, my children to be, began to form in my mind, though what a thoroughly cringe-making phrase 'we're trying for a family' is. It sounds timid, like an apology, and implies the possibility of failure (hello?). It is also an announcement to the world that your sex life has taken on a new dimension. I never actually used the phrase because of the cringe factor and also because I have always thought it sounded so old-fashioned. Bizarrely it also brings to mind an image of Les Dawson saying the words 'trying for a family' Ada style. Check out Cissie and Ada sketches on YouTube; years old, still funny.

I'm not sure that we've moved on from describing this time in a couple's life. It's still spoken of in hushed tones, but wouldn't it be better to be bold? It is surely more twenty-first century to shout from the rooftops that you're now 'bonking for a baby', 'humping for an heir', 'having a jump for a junior' or 'goosing for glory'. Whatever the phraseology to describe this time, there is always an underlying hint that some of the fun has gone from the bedroom department. After all, sex is not just for pleasure any more. It's for something much more serious – the creation of a life for God's sake. It is also most probable that blow jobs and anal sex have become a thing of the past. I told you I'd be candid.

Of course, not everyone lets on that 'trying for a family' is what they're about but when the questions referring to lack of babies start to stack up, an admission that you're trying to conceive, however you phrase it, does seem to become necessary. If the 'trying' has been going on for some time the divulgence is always with some embarrassment and is mostly received with a knowing look. The reason for the shifty whispered awkwardness, of course, is SEX and the longer the 'trying' has been going on for, the greater the possibility that the sex isn't working; something might be WRONG. Something wrong in the sex department? Possibly with the reproductive organs? Yikes, not happy talking about that at full volume; at all, in fact.

There is no need for shyness or timidity when success in this department has been achieved however, most especially if conception has occurred with ease. More of a cringe for me at that time were triumphant remarks like 'We only have to pass on the stairs and I'm up the duff again!' or 'Came off the pill and three quarters of an hour later, pregnant, just like that!'

Inevitably further down the line the 'successful sex' is announced to the world by the physical appearance of the 'bump'.

Some mums-to-be feel the need to go further and wear a T-shirt announcing their condition to the world. I remember seeing such a garment with the words 'Under Construction' emblazoned across a pregnant woman's chest with an arrow pointing down to her tummy, just in case it hadn't been noticed. Just the other day I saw a lady 'with child' in a John Lewis café wearing a T-shirt with the slogan 'Does my bump look big in this?' Ha! I smiled ruefully to myself, reflecting on how seeing this in my 'trying' days would have made my eyes well up and my stomach knot.

So, I started trying to create you in the late eighties, with a husband I should say, though not the one I'm married to now, but that's another story I'll come to later. His name was Dom – sorry *is* – he's not dead and his name is not short for Dominic as you might have thought; no his actual name is Damian. He gained the nickname Dom via the small child of a neighbour who struggled to pronounce the word Damian and instead called him Dominion (more difficult to pronounce I would have thought but hey), hence the name Dom; at least I think I've got that right.

We became friends when we were both students in Sheffield and this friendship continued post-graduation when we both started our careers in London. During this time Dom always had a girlfriend whereas I seemed to be terminally single. No one was more surprised than me when he bounced into my arms on the rebound from parting with his long-term girlfriend. I was pitched into heaven; we were happy and after a couple of years together he proposed. We were married on 13 July 1985, 'Live Aid' day. The choice of date was I suspect a huge blow for many of the guests attending our wedding; some for sure would rather have watched Saint Bob's stunning global fund raiser either on TV or attended the spectacle at Wembley Stadium but no one made it known to us and besides we weren't to know when we booked the date. Whatever, the sun shone brightly for both events.

'As much as I converse with sages and heroes, they have very little of my love and admiration. I long for a rural and domestic scene, for the warbling of birds and the prattling of my children.' John Adams, 2nd US president

We'd been married for about four years when I started to feel broody. One of my closest friends was pregnant and so was my younger brother's wife (your Aunty Alison). At the time I thought myself the typical eighties career woman strutting around central London with big hair, shoulder pads and a briefcase. It was the age of the YUPPIE (Young Upwardly Mobile Professional); as I write that out in full it sounds faintly ridiculous. I don't think I ever really qualified as a YUPPIE, as for me, the further I progressed up the career ladder the less satisfying I found my working life. Managing staff, meeting budgets and profit targets was all getting a bit meaningless. I wanted to stay at home with you doing potato prints, baking rock cakes and reading Paddington books out loud instead. These feelings increased with every birth announcement from family and friends.

When my first niece was welcomed into the world (your cousin Ellie), seeing her parents with their beautiful new baby girl and my mother with tears in her eyes as she held her first grandchild, confirmed my increasing need. So I came off the pill and we moved from north London to a 'family' home in Hertfordshire. The commute was a bit of a slog but we enjoyed the extra space and garden that living out of London afforded us, and it was so perfect for the little family we were expecting; or not as it turned out.

Of course, I took it for granted that we'd be able to conceive, I think almost everyone does. Even now I assume that the young people in my life will go on to have children, my friends becoming grandparents with ease; but with women leaving it later and later the odds against are stacking up. My track record in menstruation was a little dodgy, highly irregular and sometimes missing altogether. I later learned this is referred to as 'oligomen-orrhoea' – the first word I learned in the language of infertility. I didn't think this irregularity to be a problem, only that it meant a lot of false alarms and the purchase of a lot of expensive pregnancy tests. I spent many a morning peeing onto a white stick and willing a blue line to appear in the big window.

It did happen once, six months of 'trying' and there it was. The line was faint but it was definitely there. That would have been you, Lily. I popped the champagne in the fridge in readiness for the celebration that evening (my last drink for nine months but hey I was ecstatic). I went to work, booked a doctor's appointment and started dreaming of motherhood. By lunchtime I had started my period. I did another test the next day anyway; it was negative. I attended my appointment with the doctor regardless of the outcome but was offered little in the way of an explanation. I might have been pregnant and miscarried straight away or I may not have been pregnant at all. I was also told that the average couple takes around twelve months to conceive (that was a surprise). I was sent away to try for another six months.

Needless to say all the 'trying' was in vain and later I was referred to a gynaecologist to investigate why I hadn't conceived and so my journey on the infertility treatment trail began.

Q: What's the difference between God and a gynaecologist?
A: God doesn't think he's a gynaecologist.

I heard the above joke about halfway through my treatment and the first gynie I was under (so to speak) did, in fact, assume the role of the great man above us with the long white beard. He looked about as old too. He had white hair and an anglicised Australian accent. The god-like qualities we're talking about here are not of the loving and forgiving variety, oh no, it was more the power of creation that he was interested in.

Of course, all infertile women are hoping that the consultant they are sitting in front of can answer their prayers, so I guess it's not unreasonable for a gynaecologist to feel like God at times so I won't name him as I'm not vindictive, though for sure he's now working in that great gynaecology department in the sky; I'll call him Mr Pink. My first appointment with him was via the private sector thanks to my husband's company health care policy, something we were to be most grateful for later when the costs escalated.

We were booked in to see Mr Pink on 13 June 1990 at two o'clock. At ten minutes to three we were shown into his office – I hate people who are late. I get that from my dad, he was early for everything. I lost days as a student waiting at coach and railway stations having been dropped off 'in good time' by my father. Of course, Mr Pink's tardiness could have been down to some sort of emergency duty but this was not explained or apologised for, which I thought rude. I don't like 'rude' either, who does? I was later to learn that 'rude' was a major part of Mr Pink's make-up.

Mr Pink asked for details of our occupations. At the time I worked as Special Events Manager at the children's charity ChildLine. While I said earlier that I'd become disillusioned with my career, in fact my job at ChildLine was one I thoroughly enjoyed. I worked in the Appeals office with colleagues that were fun to work with and as the events we were organising were to raise funds for such a worthy cause, it felt rewarding and satisfying. I met many celebrities at various fund-raising events and even Princess Diana, when she came to officially open our offices in Islington. ChildLine has since become part of the NSPCC but when I worked there the charity was independent and based above a Royal Mail sorting office in Islington. I remember the ChildLine Press Officer being mighty pissed off when the tabloid coverage of Her Royal Highness's visit to our offices featured only photographs of her greeting a load of posties who had gathered outside to catch a glimpse, there was barely a mention of the work of ChildLine. I also remember Princess Di was wearing a red jacket and a black skirt; so was I. Twins!?! I also recall her perfect skin. So dewy and radiant, it was striking. My skin is not like this. I digress. Mr Pink was asking about our lifestyles; Dom was earning big bucks at Salomon Brothers, an American bank that exacted the working hours of a Victorian workhouse, but whose health care scheme was more than generous (I had heard at the time that some companies could be less than congenial when it came to fertility treatments so we were truly grateful). Mr Pink muttered something about the stressful nature of Dom's job and the fact we both commuted into London (door to door an average journey time of one and a half hours each way). I assumed it was because of the stress of commuting, it probably was, but an added factor I later learned from another source was that commuting could have an effect on male fertility in particular, something to do with sitting on the testicles for extended periods of time (not good for the spermatozoa apparently, who knew?), although as it turned out this was not a problem for my then husband.

We moved on to my menstrual history. The fact that my periods had always been irregular and sometimes lasted as long as two weeks seemed to be significant to Mr Pink but he didn't explain why. He went on to talk of the various tests I would need to undergo and the treatments available. At this point I lost him as he drifted into jargonised patter. He spouted streams of initials that I kept requesting explanations of, but in the end grew tired of asking. Initials are popular in this game, with medical personnel in general I imagine. Infertility treatment has a gamut of them, some better known than others. There's the well-known IVF, there is also GIFT, IUI, AID and AIH and probably many more I haven't heard of. I'll tell you what these initials stand for as we go along, though I fear I may cross your boredom threshold. I'll tell you one now though, SI (that's for Sexual Intercourse in case you didn't twig).

Eventually Mr Pink said that my ovaries needed a closer examination that would require minor surgery. I was unclear exactly what this involved but I later discovered, via my GP, that I was to have a laparoscopy (it sounded like something else in Australian). Mr Pink looked in his diary and suggested the following Monday – hey, no need to muck about when you're private.

When the time came I was anxious. I'd never had an operation before, never even been to hospital and I was worried that I might be one of those people who feels everything, every excruciating cut but is paralysed by the anaesthetic and unable to point this fact out. I don't know if many people have had this fear but I'm sure I'm not unique.

The admissions doctor explained the operation to me – basically a camera was to be put in my tummy to take a close look at the state of my ovaries. A short, simple explanation that surely Mr Pink could have managed, I thought. The pre-med was heaven and took away all my anxiety and down for the op I went. I was still feeling groggy when very early the next morning Mr Pink dropped by to visit me. I remember him saying my ovaries were patent. I wasn't quite sure what he meant by that. I took it to be good news; I think because the Australian pronunciation of 'patent' probably sounded like 'potent'. It wasn't good news; you only have to look up 'patent' in the *Shorter Oxford* to find that medically it means full of cysts. So bad news and there was more. I hadn't ovulated for some time. He said some other stuff as well, which I was too bleary to take in. I later learned from my GP that I had been diagnosed with Polycystic Ovary Syndrome; I didn't know what that meant either.

The vast majority of further treatments I had under Mr Pink were on the NHS and due to inevitable restrictions on the availability of expensive fertility drugs it was here that he would flex his godlike power. It became clear that it was in my best interests to be a good patient (i.e. a non-complaining compliant one) if I was to be rewarded with all those precious fertility drugs. Mr Pink and some of his staff could be quite hostile at times. He once told me of a patient of his who was getting overemotional and childish on one particular treatment programme and that (in his opinion) she'd needed a 'slap round the legs'. He also announced on one occasion that he was prepared to take less than co-operative patients off the list. Jeez! I'm sure I don't need to tell you that it was difficult *not* to become emotional almost *all* of the time. This man was prescribing large doses of hormones and then complaining of emotional women! During these times the very sight of a pregnant woman in the street could reduce me to tears, so if I was looking for a gynaecologist who could demonstrate empathy for women I was clearly in the wrong place. However, I did the compliancy bit very well.

I've done a lot of quiet compliance in my life – fitting in, doing others' bidding, pleasing people and seeking approval from others. I often wonder where the teenage girl whose school report stated 'Tessa does not take correction graciously' went. Children, please don't follow my example – it's not a good look. However, at the time to be anything other than acquiescent seemed imprudent. I bit my lip, buried my resentment towards this little man – did I say he was short? He was, and I imagine with all the little man complexes you can think of, but I became the model patient, never complaining, always cheerful and grateful. Being grateful seemed particularly important and I was, but at the same time it seemed that there was no room to be angry that this misfortune had befallen me. This emphasis also seemed to confirm that it was a situation to be ashamed of. These expensive treatments were on no account to be wasted on the ungrateful. I wasn't ill after all. I was healthy, fit and well so complaining wasn't allowed. I'd also overheard medical staff saying that women like me were a drain on resources. I told you they were hostile. I think this is where my tendency to make light of the treatment came from. It just wasn't on to make a big deal of it. Feeling compelled to behave in a way that was contrary to how I was actually feeling made me feel weak and vulnerable. I felt out of control and fragile. At this time I remember a friend of mine (with two kids) telling me how lucky I was to at least have a happy marriage and what a great husband I had. I didn't *feel* lucky and, as it turned out, didn't have the happy marriage for too much longer either.

On one occasion my patient tolerance of Mr Pink's brusque manner was severely tested. Usually I was required to telephone

Mr Pink to let him know when my period had started so that he could confirm the appropriate day to attend the hospital for scanning and drug prescription. I'd been having drug treatments and scans for around six months, which had included three false alarms and one cycle where I'd been overstimulated with the drugs. This experience had clearly thrown my body out of balance for my next period started fifteen days early and promptly stopped the very next day. I thought this worthy of a mention to Mr Pink, so I rang the hospital.

Making these calls was always difficult. ChildLine's Appeals office was open-plan and at this point I hadn't shared my infertility 'stuff' with any of my work colleagues. So I used to sneak off and find an empty office in which to make the phone call to Mr Pink – what a difference a mobile phone would have made, I could have sent him a text. I made the call and unbeknownst to me the hospital paged him while he was out walking his dog. He was furious that I'd troubled him with this 'trivial' piece of information and screamed down the phone that he had a life outside of his work and that he presumed that on some occasions even *I* took a lunch hour. Tears burned my eyes as I listened to his tirade of abuse. I was so taken aback I was reduced to an apology. An apology for a wrongdoing that was no fault of my own. I wrote to him afterwards. I was cordial, keen not to place any obstructions in the way of my treatment, and simply explained that I had *not* requested that he be paged and I suggested that he brief staff at the hospital to check when patients rang in as to whether the matter was urgent or not. He didn't acknowledge the letter. I told you he was rude.

As a result it was always with some trepidation that I made subsequent calls. I don't think Mr Pink liked women particularly, which made his career choice a bit of a puzzle or conversely it explained it. Quite frankly the man was a total twat and I'm sorry if the slang for female genitalia seems inappropriate here, but really no other word will do. I fear I might have strayed away from a certain core belief here but so what?

I am sorry to say but my experience of NHS treatment was not good. However, I don't hold the NHS responsible for this; I'm looking at you, Mr Pink. I was treated at a nearby military hospital for reasons, I presume, of available resources and convenience. I am sure that the treatment programme I received would have been the same had my local gynie been employed in a civilian hospital, though I wouldn't have been greeted by a couple of armed guards in khaki uniforms when attending appointments and treatment.

Naturally fertility treatments revolve around cycles and, with infertility patients, very often unreliable cycles. As I said before I was told when to turn up via a phone call to Mr Pink and as a result I never had a trusty appointment card to show the armed guards, so simply gaining admission onto the premises was at times fraught. On one occasion, a cold winter morning with snow falling, I was pulled over to have my car thoroughly searched. A mirror on the end of a pole was waved about beneath my car in search of explosive devices. It may sound a bit over the top but it was during the First Gulf War when it was Bush Senior's turn to bomb the bejesus out of Iraq, so security was on high alert. I waited patiently while they checked my vehicle, all the time dying for a pee. It was a requirement to arrive for a scan with a full bladder, which I will explain later – can't wait huh?! Unfortunately, the cold weather had somehow frozen the central locking system on my car and the boot would simply not open. The youth on guard didn't know what to do about it and while I knew I wasn't a terrorist threat and they knew I wasn't, still the boot had to be searched. After some considerable time waiting while the guards consulted with hospital staff I was eventually given the OK and allowed to drive on, boot unsearched. On most occasions the searches weren't so rigorous but I'm sure you can imagine the process of being questioned by a soldier with a machine gun at every appointment was unnerving. It also made me feel I had no right to be there. I needed a uniform to belong.

I'm not going to complain about the NHS; I am, in fact, a champion of our health service and will trumpet praise for it whenever I can. The provision of free medical treatment to any-one and everyone in this country is something I feel we should be immensely proud of, but NHS treatment can involve a lot of waiting, either at home, on lists, or in the corridors of hospitals. My fertility treatment was no exception and mostly, adopting my 'Mrs Compliant' persona, I didn't let it bother me. It was only when I was forced to wait with the women attending the ante-natal clinic that I struggled with the hanging around. Naturally some of the expectant mums, those that were getting close to term, were prone to whinging about aching backs, the constant round of trips to the loo, the sleepless nights and the general discomfort of being heavily pregnant. All reasonable complaints, of course, but hard to hear when you can't even get to first base. It wasn't their fault they were fertile and they weren't to know my situation, Lordy the nurses on duty didn't even know. On more than one occasion I was called up for the standard 'preg-nant woman' tests like wee samples or to have my blood pressure measured. I would then have to explain to the nurse in a room full of pregnant women that I was an *infertility* patient. The nurs-es were embarrassed, of course they were and worse, they didn't know what to do with us, the members of 'The Barren Brigade', except it seemed, to put our details at the bottom of the pile of patients' paperwork. It didn't seem to matter what time I'd arrived at the clinic, post a scan normally, it was always after *all* of the expectant mums had been seen that I would be ushered in to see Mr Pink. We had different coloured paperwork (those of us still 'trying') and I came to recognise fellow sufferers by the little green slips of paper we had detailing our drug prescriptions. It was insensitive that we, 'the bumpless', were to be treated alongside 'the expectants' but there seemed no other way around it. We were, of course, seeing the same consultant. Perhaps if the nurses were briefed to be more sympathetic it would have been easier, but hey they were working for Mr Pink don't forget.

I stuck it out with Mr Pink for eighteen months; in which time as I said earlier it was established via the laparoscopy that I had a condition called Polycystic Ovary Syndrome (PCOS). I think a little 'science bit' is required here or rather 'a biology bit' to help explain what PCOS is caused by. When during each menstrual cycle the ovaries release an egg into the uterus we're in ovulation territory; yes OK this is basic knowledge and, of course, for the normal bouncy fertile gals it occurs once a month. Before the egg is ready to be released it develops inside a tiny swelling called a follicle in the ovary. Each month, several follicles start to develop, but in most cases only one goes on to mature fully and release an egg. In PCOS, more follicles than normal are produced but often none develops enough to release an egg, with the result that ovulation does not always take place. It is basically caused by the inability of the ovaries to produce hormones in the correct proportions. There is, for example, usually far too much testosterone swilling about. Ha! No, children, I don't have a beard or a scrotum but this excess possibly explains my passion for football, my love of bad language and why I love a pint of bitter. Sadly

I am not able to bowl over arm, get a stone to skim more than three times and am rubbish at reversing a car using only the wing mirrors and various other qualities that seem to be essentially testosterone driven. I do though tend to prefer male company. I like the banter, but this might not be because of the testosterone excesses and quite possibly because of my non-mother status, or maybe I'm just a bit of a tart! I do, however, remember my father saying I'd never be a lady. I'm not sure why he said this, as I was never a tomboy, perhaps it was my inclination to clumsiness. I can picture now the tension etched on his face whenever he watched me carrying a tray of teacups. I think this quote rather sums me up:

'I have bursts of being a lady but it doesn't last long.' Shelley Winters

I've detoured from the subject rather; back to PCOS – the symptoms include: irregular or non-existent periods – tick; weight gain – may as well tick this one as it's a good excuse, though as a former disciple of the 5:2 Fast Diet this no longer applies (yay!). I say former, but it has become rather more a lifestyle than a diet and I have found my own approach to this way of living/eating and have named it the 'Kate:Nigella Principle'. However, see later for more on this, as dieting per se, or more particularly, *talking* about diets, is one of my pet hates. Excess body hair is another symptom and oh no I'm embarrassed to say I have to tick this one, though I've conquered this problem with ease via threading appointments and by making a friend of my Phillips home laser zapper thingy. Fatigue is another and I can often tick the fatigue box but just because I'm a very light sleeper and so often have disturbed nights. Depression – gladly no; acne – another embarrassed yes, though in a minor, just a few spots, sort of way; hair loss – thank God no, though when you think about it, what a mean combination of symptoms, hirsutism *and* hair loss – hair where you don't want it and at the same time it's falling out from where you do; cruel. Mood swings is another and I might as well tick that one as well, as it's a good excuse for my being grumpy whenever I am, like on those days when I feel I'm the only one in our household who empties the bin, or when Ipswich Town miss out on yet another opportunity for promotion into the Premiership, and as you know people who are late make me grouchy and rudeness in general. I could add losing internet connection, as it is common in the isolated countryside in which I now reside; I find it irritating in the extreme but nowhere near as bad as losing the TV for more than one evening. I could go on... Another side effect of PCOS is dizziness upon standing – tick. It happens to me when I get up too quickly and happens mostly when I'm gardening (a passion of mine); I can often be found leaning on my wheelbarrow or clinging to a nearby shrub, waiting for the light-headedness to subside. Final symptom: infertility – big – fat – tick.

Apparently one in five women suffer polycystic ovaries and around three quarters of them of go on to develop PCOS. It doesn't always result in infertility; it is only when the ability to ovulate has become disabled that problems occur. So, it does not automatically mean fertility disaster; many a PCOS sufferer has become a mother. I can name a couple of famous PCOS mums: Emma Thompson and Victoria Beckham, though I can't quite see where the weight gain side effect applies here, especially to the latter.

During this time I became quite an expert on conception (ironically). I thirsted for knowledge on infertility and all the available treatments. I joined two infertility charities and scoured their newsletters for new developments in treatments and to learn from other readers' experiences. There were many sad and desperate accounts; I skipped over those and focused on the stories brimming with hope and tales of joyful success. At the time of my treatment there was no internet, no World Wide Web to consult. I know for a fact that if I was having treatment now I'd be permanently online searching for miracles and like-minds. I did once phone a PCOS help line, a service provided by one of the infertility charities I belonged to. It wasn't particularly helpful because the woman answering the telephone simply wasn't a good listener. She talked about her own experience at great length and while she clearly empathised with me and made me realise I wasn't suffering alone with the problem, she made two mistakes. The first was to tell me that I was lucky to have been diagnosed fairly early on in my treatment; she hadn't been apparently. Again I wasn't feeling 'lucky'. The other problem was the intrusion of a baby crying in the background (she'd just adopted). It seemed churlish not to share her joy (she was clearly thrilled) but I think it might have been a good idea for her to stop manning the help line at that point.

So Mr Pink established the reason I had not been able to conceive; a start at least. It was also established that Dom was Mr Super Sperm, a slight exaggeration but certainly all was well in the 'baby batter' department. So, all my fault then. Actually that fact suited me, as male infertility has such an unfortunate connection with virility. We really need a role model on the male infertility scene to help reverse this. A big macho guy to be a bit short of lead in the old pencil. A sexy, good-looking 'jaffa' would certainly help remove the association. Some male figures have been associated with fertility charities, Chris de Burgh is one, he is a patron of Infertility Network UK; umm, not the Brad

Pitt/Liam Neeson/Idris Elba we need I feel. The trouble is, it just doesn't work does it? We can't use an infertile guy to explode the virility myth. Fertility is, and I fear always will be, something to beat the male chest about. So I feel especially sorry for the men who have fertility issues, the 'starting pistols' silently feeling less of a man. It's interesting I think that in the only paragraph I've written on male infertility, I've used two slang terms 'jaffa' (seedless) and 'starting pistol' (firing blanks), and yet I don't know of one decent slang word for the infertile female. Perhaps I should invent one.

I love slang words. Flicking through my slang dictionary is one of my favourite things to do; it just makes me laugh to see swear words followed by a definition presented so formally. I find it hilarious the sheer number of words we have for the male member, for the vagina and for breasts; some of the words make me laugh out loud, usually the Australian versions.

Sadly not too many laughs were to be had under the 'care' of the Australian gynaecologist. During my time with Mr Pink, I had seventeen treatment cycles, six false alarms and two threats to take me off the treatment programme – costs were always blamed. The second threat was enough to force me to take refuge in the private sector, again an option paid for by the American bank Dom worked for. Mr Pink was a gynaecologist and not a fertility expert and often seemed frustrated by the refusal of my body to respond appropriately to the treatments he prescribed and to be fair I had also run out of drug treatment options. IVF was beckoning and since during the late eighties/early nineties it wasn't an option readily available on the NHS, we had to go private.

I was referred to the Portland Hospital, London, in March 1992 exactly three years after we had started 'trying'. It was at the Portland I met gynaecologist number two on my treatment trail. He was a lot younger than Mr Pink and a bit of a David Suchet lookalike though without the Hercule Poirot moustache (thankfully). I was also looked after from time to time by his colleague. He was a Nigel Havers lookie–likie, which I found a little unnerving since at the time the actor was in a television series called *The Charmer* playing the role of a seducer and murderer. I don't think either of these gynaecologists thought of themselves as god-like particularly and, of course, because I was paying there was no whinging about expensive drugs or idle threats to withdraw treatment. This wasn't like visiting a medical establishment or a military one; it was more like a middle range hotel. I had swapped cold and hostile hospital corridors for welcoming thick pile, navy-blue carpets with bland watercolour pictures and pot plants. On one of my visits to the hospital it appeared that I'd also swapped the khaki clad armed guards for members of the paparazzi. They were waiting for the appearance of Rod Stewart with whichever leggy blonde model he was with at time and, of course, their new golden-haired child. They looked up as I appeared at the doors of the Portland and, of course, quickly away again when it became clear that some no-mark was leaving the building. It occurred to me then, how much more difficult it would be to undergo fertility treatment as a celebrity.

In the main reception area a framed photograph of another pair of famous parents was proudly displayed, a family portrait of the Duke and Duchess of York. They split up shortly after my referral to the Portland and the photograph was replaced with one that just featured the Duchess with her daughters; well, it happens to the best of us. There were also photos of babies on a noticeboard outside the fertility consultant's office. It was crowded with them and the accompanying letters and cards of gratitude. Of course, I longed for the day when a photo of you, my precious babies, would be pinned there alongside my thank-you card.

The difference I most appreciated in the private sector was that the atmosphere was sympathetic. The plush surroundings were, of course, conducive to a more pleasant experience but mostly it felt better because I wasn't the oddball, no longer the bumpless outsider with the green paperwork. I was never asked by other patients, or by nursing staff, when my baby was due (this happened to me once in the NHS antenatal waiting room – was it because I was wearing a baggy jumper or did I just look like I was suffering from the weight gain side effect of PCOS?). No matter, now it felt like I was among friends. Of course, I was paying; it makes a difference. Many of the drugs had to be paid for in advance. I swear you could not leave the building with so much as an Elastoplast without a receipt.

My private treatment began with similar drug treatments to those I had under Mr Pink, though more carefully and accurately monitored because of better equipment. In simple terms the treatment mainly comprised of lots of drug taking, lots of blood tests, urine samples, scans, scans and more scans with the odd surgical procedure thrown in and with a copious use of initials to label each procedure; as I said before they're popular in gynaecology, I guess it's because of all those long words. I mentioned before the use of SI for Sexual Intercourse – you might have thought I was joking. I wasn't. On one occasion the David Suchet lookalike was dictating my latest treatment programme to his secretary while I waited for some paperwork. It was post the first failure of an IVF treatment and I was to take a break from all the injectable drugs and to 'try' for a month or two on the simpler treatment regimen of just oral drugs. He mentioned the drug name and then said the initials SI. 'SI', I thought, what's that? I said nothing (luckily) and then it dawned on me. Sexual Intercourse! That old chestnut. We'd long since given up on that as a means of making a baby.

—❧❧—

I used to refer to these times as being on 'The Treatment Treadmill', as that was how it was beginning to feel. I mentioned scans and blood tests; there were also a lot of injections; lots and lots of injections. Luckily injections didn't bother me too much, just as well, but (although it's a bit mean) I do like this quote:

'Injections are the best thing ever invented for feeding doctors.'
Gabriel Garcia Marquez

Under Mr Pink scans took place at the military hospital and, as I have said before, this required attendance with my bladder full. The bladder needed to be full so as to push the ovaries close to the surface of the tummy so that a clear picture of what was going on in the ovaries could be viewed. Sometimes my bladder wasn't full enough to get a clear picture so I was required to sit and wait while sipping from a large glass of water. On the 'water torture' as one scanner jokingly referred to it. Though I had no idea of his rank, I imaginatively nicknamed him 'Sergeant Scan'. Often as not the wait seemed an eternity. The department didn't work on a first come first served basis. It was soldiers first, then the pregnant ones, then us, the green paperwork ladies; we were always, it seemed to me, last. Sorry if I'm sounding a bit 'poor me' here or even ever so slightly paranoid, but it seemed that our needs were simply not accommodated for.

The purpose of these scans (when there is definitely no baby inside you) is to look at the egg follicles to see how they're growing. When you're being pumped full of hormones it's important not to administer too many otherwise overstimulation can take place. It still does sometimes; it happened to me once or twice but I felt no ill effects, mostly it just meant that the month's treatment had been a waste of time. For others the consequences can be life threatening so it is a situation to be taken seriously. From the scan the follicles are measured and when they reach the optimum size (around twenty millimetres) an injection of an ovulation-inducing hormone called Human Chorionic Gonadotrophin (HCG) is prescribed to prompt ovulation. Amusing isn't it, to find that 'gonad' forms part of this term?

Scanning in private health care was much different, not only because, obviously, there was no waiting with injured soldiers or mums-to-be but also because different equipment was used. Private health care meant internal scans.[2] No full bladder required just a probe not unlike a dildo inserted into the vagina (where else). This provided a clear picture on the screen of the follicles growing (or otherwise) in the ovaries. Before using the vaginal ultrasound equipment, a condom would be freed from its foil packaging and used to cover the probe, a procedure I always found faintly amusing. I'm sure Durex wouldn't have had infertility clinics in mind as top buyers of their products, but they must get through tons of them.

It also occurred to me while having these internal scans (and there were a lot of them) that gynies might recognise their patients by their labia rather than their facial features. I often wondered if they would think to themselves

'Oh here's Mrs Fluffy-Muff again', or 'Mrs Ginger-Minge' or 'Oh yes I know this patient, it's the old beef curtains again.' Brazilians back in my treatment days would simply have been someone who hailed from Brazil.

The scans were not pleasant, lying there legs akimbo while trying to be relaxed and casual about the fact a complete stranger is wiggling an object shaped like a vibrator inside your velvet tardis is not an activity I'd recommend. I hardly need impress that it was in no way sexual; in fact, I think you'd struggle to get further away from the arousal end of the scale, especially when

---

[2] Nowadays the NHS also provides internal scans.

you're wondering how your front bottom compares to that of the previous patient.

Luckily I don't recall feeling any anxiety about the appearance of my Lady Garden at the time and I think thanks are due to *Cosmopolitan* for this peace of mind since I recall way back a double page spread (of spreads?!) in the magazine with photographs of around fifty vaginas; the variety of shapes and sizes of which was extraordinary. I remember the comfort and reassurance that came from glancing over the images and thinking 'ah there's mine'.

At the time of my fertility treatment I had adopted a laissez-faire approach to this department, as Gwyneth Paltrow calls it a '70s vibe', which probably says rather more than I'd care to admit about how I was feeling about my body at the time. Since those days I have felt a need to tend my bush into a more fashionable style and for a while like many other women did sport a 'landing strip'. I think that phase was due to a kind of 'mid-life thang' and quite frankly it was an awful faff to maintain. Obviously, I'm talking mainly to Lily here, though hang on a minute, it might be good for you boy(s) too, if it's not too much of a cringe. Of course, you do not need to know that I am now comfortable with a small neat and tidy triangle and I'm certainly not asking you to imagine your mother attached to medical apparatus with parted thighs, but it might be good for you to know some of this 'stuff' should you ever need to relate to a woman with 'vag angst'.

Neither is this the place to enter the arena of whether women should or should not groom their bits to be more 'feminine' or sexy but I hope, Lily, that you wouldn't feel the pressure to vajazzle (if only to avoid the risk of infection) or indeed to have cosmetic surgery to 'improve' the appearance of your genitalia. By all means grab a vaginoplasty procedure if, later in life, everything has gone a bit slack and you've found yourself in 'waving a sausage in the Albert Hall' territory (or indeed for any other medical grounds), but surgery for purely cosmetic reasons? I don't think so. I'll just take my judge's wig off here and concede to those genuinely debilitated by the appearance of their pudenda and those suffering major discomfort, but to glibly opt for a surgical procedure, which could result in blunt unfeeling scar tissue replacing all those sensitive nerve endings that highlight and extend sensation, is beyond belief. We rightly campaign for the cessation of the most abhorrent of practices, female genital mutilation, but at the same time, carve up our own for vanity. Are we mad? Here endeth my very own 'Vagina Monologue'.

The scan, as I said, is to check out what's going on in the ovary department depending on what part of the cycle you're at. Some of the gynies would do the scans themselves; others had staff specifically employed for the job. Sometimes I would be shown the screen with an explanation as to what was what, how big the follicles were etc.; on other occasions I would just lie there and be told nothing about what was going on inside my body. Back at the military hospital Sergeant Scan never explained anything, his female equivalent always did. In the private sector it varied too, the David Suchet lookalike didn't, the Nigel Havers did. Mr Pink didn't perform scans, which was probably a good thing.

From the onset fertility treatment for most people requires the administration of various drugs. In the early days of my treatment the drugs I took were mainly in tablet form and their purpose to help ovulation. The main one and the cheapest (so a major player in the NHS) is clomiphene[3] (brand name Clomid),

---

[3] This is still so today.

which stimulates the natural release of a follicle-stimulating hormone (FSH). I was sometimes prescribed cyclofenil, a similar drug to Clomid. I remember the first occasion I was prescribed it vividly because the pharmacist hadn't heard of it and I'd had to explain to him (in my very crowded local Boots) what it was for. This infertility business seemed to be forever attracting awkward and embarrassing situations.

When I first started taking Clomid I was required to take my temperature regularly and when it went up (a sign that ovulation is about to occur) we'd bonk and hope. My temperature charts didn't ever markedly go up or down so that idea was soon ditched and I moved on to combining Clomid with an injection of HCG. As I said earlier the HCG was administered once the follicles had grown big enough. So I would take the Clomid and then usually several scans later (meaning many tiresome and time-consuming visits to hospitals or clinics) I'd get a jab of HCG to make me ovulate. Once the drug combination hadn't worked for a few cycles the Clomid was dumped for a jab of another hormone, HMG (Human Menopausal Gonadotrophin), so I was now on a drug regimen that required both the drugs to be injected and both with the word gonad in the name. I got pretty used to needles during this time, but some nurses were definitely more adept at administering the drugs than others. One thing that did not vary was that they were always administered to the same place – the buttock. Again too there was a difference between the NHS and private. As you might expect NHS treatment was long and involved; private was quick and easy. At the private clinic I would be shown into a comfy room and with minimal fuss a nurse would give me the jab and off I'd pop back to work.

The NHS was a different story. From the scanning department of the military hospital I attended I would normally be sent off to Ward Six where I would hover outside the nurses' station and then tentatively ask (the Mrs Compliant persona firmly in place) if there was a nurse available to give me an injection. I'd then be instructed to wait in the corridor. The corridor if I was lucky, sometimes I had to go to the day room to wait for my jab. More often than not this required walking through a ward of wounded young soldiers. It was a bit like walking past a building site, though without the banter and wolf whistles. I would then take my seat among a gathering of injured or sick military personnel watching daytime telly.

On one occasion the room was occupied by a man with a badly smashed-up face who was being remarkably cheerful, most likely for the benefit of the relatives who surrounded him. There was also a chap with a sort of foam-and-steel-splint arrangement supporting his arm. He looked grim and was clearly in some discomfort. I felt like an intruder in their misfortune and their recovery, sitting there in my rude health with all of them (I imagined) wondering what the hell I was doing there. Often I'd wait for an hour or more, the delay often caused by the simple fact they had none of the drug I required in the ward's pharmacy. Hardly surprising since injured soldiers have little use for hormone injections to aid their recovery. I once offered to go and collect the drug from the hospital's main pharmacy myself but, of course, that was against procedure. Once the drug was located I would be asked to remove all my lower body clothes (the infertility nurses at the Portland just asked me to hitch my knickers up a bit), then I would get up on to a couch and be given my injection. Clinging to my dignity I would get dressed and usually there followed a discussion as to what they were to do with my paperwork. I didn't know where the slip of green paper, which detailed how many ampoules of the drug I'd just had administered, was to be filed, and mostly nor did they.

It wasn't the nurses' fault, of course, and mostly they were kind. Unfortunately, I just remember the ones that weren't. Some asked about the treatment; I remember one asking me, stifling a giggle, if I was to now go home and 'do it'. Another suggested I went home and bought a dog; the drugs were so expensive, you see. I didn't want a dog; I wanted you.

The 'dog' remark somehow invalidated how I was feeling. That particular nurse's lack of empathy made what was happening to me feel small, perhaps I shouldn't have been making such a big deal about it and yet this thing was enormous to me. To hear someone making light of it, being flippant about it, was crushing. Those sorts of remarks just served to drive people like me underground. It's the same as saying 'Chin up!' to someone with depression.

As I said earlier the HCG injection was to stimulate ovulation. Clearly that's when you're in business. When the HCG drug was mentioned on your green slip of paper it meant go home and bonk. Mr Pink, the Aussie twat, would actually prescribe a time. It didn't seem to matter what time I'd had my jab, six o'clock the following morning was the designated time for sex. Was he having a laugh? I mean I know it's not unusual for a man to wake up with a stiffy but when it has to be at a precise time and after your wife has had umpteen scans, blood tests and injections, it's a pressure. Credit to Dom, he did always manage it, though at times it must have felt like a chore. Obviously, it wasn't spontaneous and if we'd felt horny the night before we dare not waste the sperm in case the egg wasn't ready and waiting. Apparently even Super Sperm don't have the capacity to hang around for too long waiting for a ripened egg to appear. For me, of course, it was simply a chance that we might make a precious baby. The quality of the sex I have to admit was mattering less and less to me. I realise I'm on taboo ground here telling my children about my sex life; of course, you would have been spared this had you come into my life.

How was Dom feeling at this time? I am ashamed to admit I can't honestly say; did I ever really know? I think subsequent events have distorted how I view our relationship at this time. I'm sure he still loved me then and was hurt by my pain; our pain, but as I write these words doubts are crowding in. Did he really want to become your father? Did he ever want to have a family with me? I simply don't know the answer to that but I fear the quest to have you had become all about *me*; the treatment so all-consuming that attention to his needs, his suffering, became second place. I knew that at times he felt lost and helpless and just a bit useless, sitting on the side-lines watching me endure all sorts of procedures. He was always kind and supportive; I'm not sure that I was the same to him. I don't do regrets; I did the best I could with what I had at the time, but I am wiser now and have learned greater empathy for others. Something I would have hoped to pass on to you.

As it turned out I think Mr Pink was having a laugh. The Portland gynies suggested intercourse could take place *anytime* over the following forty-eight hours post an HCG injection. The suggestion was always discreet and, of course, in private. Not so with Mr Pink, he would suggest having intercourse (not with him, obviously) in a loud voice in the waiting room. Jeez!

There was another drug treatment that I was prescribed on two occasions that I was required to inhale. It was some sort of hormonal correction thingy and it was called Buserelin. I remember its name nearly three decades later without looking it up; this is because it was the most inconvenient method of administering drugs I'd come across and this coming from someone who had regular injections in her bottom, though I would ask asthma and allergy sufferers to forgive my petulance. The purpose of this drug was to switch off my natural production of the hormones controlling the development of the eggs. This would, in turn, allow the ovaries to become more receptive to the hormones given by injection. I was to inhale the Buserelin five times a day for between three to five weeks. Dedicated to taking my drugs properly, desperate not to cock up the treatment, I made every effort to sniff at the appointed hour but I drew the line at setting the alarm for a dose in the middle of the night. Taking Buserelin drove me mad; I regularly forgot to take the inhaler with me when I went out and every time I forgot it I berated myself for possibly messing up the odds on conception.

Whether hormones were being inhaled or injected, blood and urine tests were always a feature and were done at regular intervals to check out what was going on with my hormones. Like the administration of the drugs, the skill of the person taking the blood made an enormous difference to the pain level. I did on one occasion end up feeling a little faint when a nurse with the needle in my arm kept wiggling it around to find a vein until I ended up with a massive bruise that looked like a miniature dartboard with the hole in my skin as the bull's eye. On my many trips to the blood-taking department I would sit and wait outside the treatment cubicles willing a certain Filipina nurse to call my name. She was an expert, a sublime phlebotomist. I can honestly say I rarely felt a thing. I never told her how good she was, which was remiss of me, for seeing her face on treatment days made it all so much easier.

The urine tests were less frequent and, of course, required little more than developing a straight aim when filling the little plastic sample bottles. Again they were testing for the presence of various hormones. After filling the sample bottle, for some reason I always found the warmth of the bottle disconcerting. Why was that I wonder? I mean we all pee. I would find myself wondering if the colour was OK – should it have been paler? Should I have been aiming for a pale straw-coloured pee or something more lemon sorbet?

Another crucial test in the establishment of why a pregnancy isn't happening is the all-important sperm test. Of course, I can only tell you what Dom told me. Again there was a difference on the NHS to private. At the military establishment he was given a pot and directed to the lavatories! Very conducive. In the private sector you could do it at home if you wished and pop it back to them later. It was an embarrassing business; of course it was, we are talking about masturbation here, and quite naturally there are a lot of old jokes associated with this area, like the one where the man giving a sample ('the wanker' we could call him) asks the blonde nurse with big tits for assistance. There are also rumours that dirty magazines are provided for inspiration. This wasn't the case for my husband, no well-thumbed copy of *Penthouse* for him; he had to use his own imagination. In view of later events I won't go there but whatever his motivation he passed the tests with an A*.

Talking of masturbation it puts me in mind of a documentary I saw many years ago investigating the female orgasm. I wonder how many hands went up when that research job was proposed – so to speak! It was demonstrated that the female orgasm helped the sperm on their way to their destination, that being the egg. It occurred to me that it might be worth researching for use post IUI (Intra-Uterine Insemination – insemination directly into the uterus). Masturbating to aid conception – a bizarre idea perhaps and I guess it would be subject to abuse, medical students peeking through curtains, pervy doctors offering assistance and so on. I imagine too it would only be an option available in the private sector, no pleasure on the NHS; no wankers either?

I was to learn a lot about the human reproductive system and was told many a time how inefficient us humans are at reproducing compared to other species. We are apparently second only to pandas. This isn't helped by the fact that many women have little understanding as to how their bodies work; no knowledge of when ovulation normally occurs or what the signs of ovulation are. To me the unplanned pregnancies are the miracles and were also the hardest for me to cope with in others. It was difficult enough to hear of the wanted pregnancies of family and friends during this time but those that were not planned for were even harder. When a friend found herself pregnant when she didn't want to be it was a difficult situation for both of us. I found it hard to give advice and support to someone who wanted to get rid of something that I was aching to have. It was a decision I knew that I would never have to make.

I should also say that at this time, the treatment programme was dominating my life. ChildLine were the most sympathetic employers but I was having so much time off for appointments that I felt uneasy. I felt guilty too. I was working for a charity after all. So I decided to work part-time to try to ease the situation, but my job description remained the same, so the outcome was effectively cramming five days' work into three and being paid less for it. Plus, of course, not all the appointments were conveniently on my days off so it was still eating into my work time. After a few months part-time I left ChildLine and worked freelance for a while. I also did some voluntary work with a local nursery for disadvantaged children, but sadly found it too harrowing. Being with children didn't soothe me as I had hoped it might, it made the ache to have my own even harder to bear.

When the ascent on the IVF mountain began, I stopped work altogether. We also decided to move back to London, well Kew, not London but a shorter commute for Dom. They say 'new house, new baby' so I was full of hope. Our second ideal 'family' home seemed perfect. There was a delightful primary school just up the road, Kew Gardens just a five-minute walk away and a young family living next door. The house needed a lot of work doing to it so I spent my work-free days organising plumbers, electricians, kitchen-fitters and carpenters to transform our home. I also attended a part-time interior design course in near-by Richmond for inspiration and distraction. I kept myself busy, but all the time I was praying for the glorious day when Dom and I would bring you home.

With hindsight I think packing up my career added to the pressure and tension of the situation. All of my contemporaries were giving up work to actually *have* a baby, while I was just dreaming of you. I felt guilty too. While I was adding value to our home, decorating and doing small DIY jobs, essentially it felt like I wasn't contributing any more. I was wishing my life away, watching and waiting through every menstrual cycle, looking for signs that never came. I was totally focused on one aim and it wasn't healthy.

So, IVF was next, in-vitro fertilisation – a test-tube baby.

'No test tube can breed love and affection. No frozen packet of semen ever read a story to a sleepy child.' Shirley Williams

Fairly obvious I think, Shirley, but I think we know what she means here.

Statistics vary from clinic to clinic, but the average number of successful IVF procedures at my time of treatment was a lofty 10 per cent. Given those odds it's a wonder people even attempted it. Success rates are better now than they were in the early nineties: up to a quarter for women in their early thirties, petering off to the 10 per cent range when over forty. That said it still remains a mystery to me as to why the media portray IVF as such an easy option. Yes, the miracle baby stories abound and are celebrated, alongside the articles condemning those 'too old for motherhood', but whatever your age or circumstance, believe me, even now the IVF road is a very hard one to travel.

Having said that IVF for those who are fertile is easier I believe. Puzzled? IVF for the fertile? Yes I thought so, but more and more single women are using it as a way to get a longed-for child, having given up on the traditional, meet the child's father first route. I should probably put on my non-judging hat here, as I have never taken a step wearing the moccasins of a single fertile woman. Neither have I walked in the shoes of a child who will never know who his or her father is. All I will say is, I wanted a *family* not just a baby.

What about the single man too? The broody singleton male exists, surely he does? It's clearly not so easy for him to have his own biological child. Obviously, he would have to find and pay for a surrogate, unless he has a friend or family member willing to oblige. Whereas the single gal needs but a turkey baster or can simply shag a passer-by. Of course, I'm being flippant here, it's not a decision ever taken that lightly, is it? I mean, ahem, a woman wouldn't 'mug' a man for his sperm, would she? Would she?

—☙❦❧—

The treatment background to IVF is very similar to the one I have already detailed on the treatment trail, in that drugs are administered to promote follicle growth that in turn goes on to produce eggs. Again progress of the growth of the follicles is carefully monitored via ultrasound and then followed by an HCG jab to bring on ovulation. The difference is, post the HCG injection, rather than leaving the eggs to meet up with the sperm inside the body, the eggs are removed and are mixed with the sperm outside the body, i.e. 'in the test tube'. Also with IVF more eggs are required to increase the odds on getting enough fertilised, so much higher doses of the drugs are required. All the eggs have to be removed; in my case they were removed via a laparoscopy under general anaesthetic. They aren't always; some are done under local anaesthetic with ultrasound. The eggs are then introduced to the sperm and hopefully a fertilisation takes place. The fertilised embryos are then placed inside the womb where, if things go well, one will implant (it was a maximum of three embryos when I was being treated, it is now usually two). There are presently moves to allow only one embryo to be placed inside to avoid multiple pregnancies and the risks this entails. I don't mean this letter to become a discussion document on the ethics of IVF treatment so I'll say no more, other than to say that when the odds are stacked against you, as they so often are in this business, to reduce them even further would, for me, be difficult to accept.

When I was being treated at the Portland egg collection took place on day twelve of the cycle and this was not possible if day twelve happened to land on a weekend. So basically if my period started on a Tuesday or a Wednesday I was not eligible for the treatment in that cycle. After it had been decided that IVF was the next step for us, my next period did start on a Tuesday. At first I was relieved. This may surprise you but I was becoming increasingly anxious about the whole procedure. However, when I checked the calendar and realised that my next cycle would probably coincide with Christmas my mood changed. If the gynies weren't able to front-up for an egg collection on a weekend they sure as hell weren't going to put in an appearance on Christmas Eve. This meant waiting yet another month. Another Christmas and New Year with no baby on the horizon. There was nothing I could do about it so Christmas was celebrated and the New Year welcomed in, again with renewed hope that this year (1993) would be THE YEAR. It was to be our fifth year of trying and, as it turned out, our last.

In early January, my period ever so slightly started on a Wednesday, so I lied and said it was the Thursday and booked an appointment at the Portland. The David Suchet gynie had a look around via the vaginal ultrasound and everything was looking good, so I had got away with it. I was given a consent form to sign, which stated that I'd had the whole process explained to me and that I was also aware that a counsellor was available to me should I need one. None of this was actually the case. Despite some explanation of the procedure I was still unsure as to whether I was to undergo the ultrasound or laparoscopic method of egg collection and I hadn't been offered a counsellor either. Why hadn't I asked for clarification? Why didn't I point out that counselling hadn't been mentioned? To be honest I didn't think I needed any counselling and as to why I didn't ask about the procedure itself I can only say that I was feeling raw and anxious and always found it difficult to come away with all the facts. Children, if you ever have to attend a medical consultation of any kind, I would advise going armed with a notebook[4] in which you have previously written down a list of all your queries and then endeavour to make sure that you don't leave the building until all of them have been answered and those answers written down.

---

[4] Notebook! Ha! I guess you wouldn't use such a thing; use the Notes app on your phone.

I signed the consent form and came away presuming I was to have the ultrasound method of egg collection, I'd read it was more common. I'd also read that there was *some* discomfort; how much exactly I wondered? I mean was it going to be bloody painful? I went home with a stash of drugs to store in my fridge and lots of unanswered questions.

What had been made clear was that the procedure was to include an injection every day from day four of the cycle until day ten, so seven jabs in all; some I arranged to have at my local GP's surgery which made life easier, but for most of them I had to travel my old commuter route to the Portland[5] where I also had regular scans to check on the follicle growth. During this time my overriding feeling was that I just wanted to get it over with. IVF was what everyone talked about. It had worked for thousands of people blah blah blah. As I said before no one seemed to realise that the chances of success, especially for a first timer, were extremely low. There were still lots of unanswered questions. Would I produce enough eggs, any eggs? Would they get along OK with the sperm, or could the biochemistry between them be problematic? I felt I should be positive but I was struggling. I hated the round of constant injections, hated the idea of having so many drugs pumped into me coupled with the regular prodding and poking around of the most intimate parts of my body. I felt weak and trapped. What was I to do, give up the treatment and give up on you? What choice was there when there was no choice at all? I had to keep going.

Since I was struggling to keep it together Dom came with me for my scanning appointment on day nine (a Friday) to support me

---

[5] Nowadays patient are allowed to administer their own injections, which at least would remove the inconvenience if not the taboo.

and to help ascertain exactly what procedure I would be having. I had my internal scan in the consultant's office, while Dom was left sitting in a chair with his back to me. The scan indicated all was progressing well and that we were on schedule for egg collection on the following Monday. I also learned that I was to have laparoscopic egg collection; I was to be out sparko while they collected the eggs, which was a huge relief. Prior to the egg collection I was to have an injection of HCG, to send a message to the ovary to start getting ready to fire the egg out. The timing of this procedure was interesting. I was to attend the Portland for an injection at midnight the following day, a Saturday – for God's sake! We'd got people coming for the weekend. We'd planned a big night out. This whole bloody business was taking over our lives.

Our friends stayed on the Friday night but they made other plans for the Saturday. It was awkward, but I couldn't face coming back to a house full of people post a trip into central London for a midnight rendezvous with a needle full of HCG. I wished I could have been more relaxed and not let it prevent us from behaving normally but the procedure itself created too much tension.

We arrived at the Portland and as directed went up to one of the wards to get the jab done and waited patiently on some seats beside the nurses' station. Another couple, clearly in the same boat, were waiting too. We smiled awkwardly at each other while both us gals waited for our injections. They were an oriental couple and I remember saying to Dom if we get a Chinese looking baby we'll know they've made a mistake, which, of course, was a bit of an impossibility because we weren't having our eggs collected, but we were clearly on the same timetable. In view of reported mix-ups that have come to light in recent years, it wasn't such a joke.

The following Monday brought good news. I had the procedure in the blissful ignorance of general anaesthetic, and joy – they'd collected twelve eggs. A huge relief, I had been obsessing that I wouldn't manage any at all. The next hurdle, of course, was to establish whether, with my husband's contribution, they could become fertilised. The IVF nurse, herself pregnant at the time – difficult for me but, of course, not her fault – told me that she would call me at 11.30 the following morning to let me know if fertilisation had occurred. After almost a day of my sitting on top of the telephone she eventually called with the news that four eggs had shown signs of fertilisation and that I should report back to the clinic the next day to have three embryos put back. Of course, I was relieved that some had fertilised but at the same time I was disappointed that there weren't any extras to bung in the freezer for another crack at it, should it not work this time. That was the trouble with the process: every hurdle cleared, one's expectations rose; just a week prior I would have been happy to hear of *one* egg showing signs of fertilisation. Now I was disappointed with four.

Having the eggs replaced is not such a big deal, rather like an over-elaborate smear test. Ice-cream scoop inserted, jacked open and the little critters squirted in. I only had two embryos replaced in the end because two hadn't fertilised successfully. Afterwards I was required to lie still for thirty minutes. I was afraid to move. In fact, I was almost afraid to move for the next three days. The gynie had told me to take it easy for a week and then to return to business as usual. I felt frozen in a limbo land of escalating, dizzying hopes coupled with a hard fear and dread of failure.

My period was due on around fourteen days post the HCG injection but I had been warned that the timing could be a bit messed up because of the egg collection. I surrounded myself with books and magazines, banned alcohol and caffeine and sat on the sofa sipping water and chewing on healthful fruit, nuts and seeds, enveloped in a big bubble of hope.

The day before my period was due I had the strongest feeling that I wasn't pregnant. I kept it to myself. When I was proved to be right the very next day I was in a state of shock. While I'd thought that it probably hadn't worked, that you weren't implanting but slipping away, deep down I still hoped that it had. Hoped that at last you were on your way to me. It was shattering. I couldn't take it in at first. I put the kettle on, my standard crisis procedure, and then I wept. Big, howling, fat wet tears. I sat alone at my kitchen table, nursing a mug of tea and let all the tension and stress of the past few weeks pour out through my tears. The next difficulty was that it had to be *me* who had to tell everybody that it hadn't worked, including Dom. I hated the fact that *I* always had to be the first to know. Why couldn't someone break it to me gently, instead of my making a miserable visit to the loo to confirm the worst?

I have a vivid snapshot in my head of this time – I am seated on the floor in our sitting room at Dom's feet. My head is on his knee and he is stroking my hair. The sound of REM's 'Everybody Hurts' is ringing out from the CD player – the lyrics and tone filling the room and capturing our mood completely. It was a precious tender moment that was both uplifting and reassuring. But my body had failed us yet again and we knew that soon we'd be facing the whole process once more.

The release of the tension lifted me for a day or two, sufficient to be cheerful to family and friends. I went back to see the David Suchet lookalike and he suggested another try in April. It was then early February. The next bash was to be via GIFT. I'd always loved the term 'GIFT', it felt so appropriate; it actually stands for Gamete Intra-Fallopian Transfer and the procedure is much the same as for IVF. It entails the usual drugs, scans, drugs, scans, more drugs and more scans until such point as the eggs are produced. The eggs are collected in the same way but instead of being fertilised in the test tube, both the eggs and sperm are placed into the fallopian tube before fertilisation. So the main difference being that fertilisation takes place where nature intended it to happen – hopefully. And that's a big hopefully.

I wasn't quite sure why I'd been put forward to have GIFT because I've looked it up on t'internet since and it doesn't even look like I was an appropriate candidate for the treatment, but as you read on you'll find that whether I was or not became academic. Nevertheless it is disturbing to learn that at times it was possible that I didn't get prescribed the appropriate treatment. It wasn't the only time it had happened. I remember on one occasion under Mr Pink I was prescribed the drug to induce ovulation too early. I knew it was the wrong time because of the follicle measurements written on my green slip of paper; the biggest one was only fourteen millimetres. I knew it had to be larger than that, but Mr Pink was unavailable and a stand-in for him had prescribed the HCG. I didn't feel able to correct a professional. I was, as ever, reduced to muteness for fear of offence, or withdrawal of treatment. I've touched on this before; it was a factor throughout my treatment that I didn't feel able to ask pertinent questions or for clarification when I was confused. I felt like a victim, albeit a willing victim as I just accepted the decisions without question. I seemed to lack the energy and the confidence to ever press home my own point of view. I put it down to the sheer desperation of it all.

Post the IVF failure I learned that some of my eggs were chromosomally abnormal – great. I wasn't quite sure what it meant but apparently they could sort the problem out with yet more drugs – so that was all right then. It was at this time that I was introduced to the nasal spray Buserelin. It's hard to imagine how a nasal spray can affect hormone production. For hay fever sufferers, a nasal spray feels a natural enough solution but as an indirect means to get pregnant? Hardly. I just inhaled it in sweet oblivion. I have since learned that it is not for those with polycystic ovary disease, so that's a bit of a puzzle. However, it can be used in the treatment of endometriosis, as it later turned out I had a spot of that, so maybe it did me some good. As I said before, the purpose of the spray is to switch off the natural hormones that control the release of eggs from the ovaries, in order that the administered ones will have a clean slate to work from as it were. Whatever, I was sent home with an inhaler to use every five hours for three weeks and also some Clomid so we could have a couple of semi-natural bashes at conception – using the SI method!

Around this time I slumped into something of a depression and began to overeat, which annoyed me because just before the IVF attempt I'd received my Weight Watchers badge of honour for reaching my target weight. Funny that I should join Weight Watchers at a time when my real desire was to become hugely fat with you growing inside of me, but as weight gain was a symptom of PCOS it was recommended to shift some of it. I wasn't massively overweight, never have been really, but I have carried a bit of extra timber from time to time so I was glad when I managed to shed a stone and a half to reach my Weight Watchers target weight. As a result I actually became a bit obsessed with my weight at this time and I blame Weight Watchers for that.

I know things have changed since then, but I'd like to share a little of my experience of this particular slimming club, circa 1990. First the weigh-in at the start of every meeting (still a requirement I understand) lining up in a long queue waiting to be weighed. It was the middle of winter and I noticed that a lot of the women (in fact, it was solely women attending, not a man in sight) wore the same clothes every week. Two very large ladies were wearing light cotton dresses, which struck me as odd; it was winter, it was cold outside. I assumed that this was either because the clothing simply weighed less or perhaps that they had joined Weight Watchers in the summer and their weight might be up a pound or two if they put a cardi on. Another factor in the weigh-in (bearing in mind we are talking small increments of weight loss or gain) is, to be quite blunt, whether you've managed to have a damn good 'Forrest Gump' before you attend class. I discovered that a perfectly timed laxative could make the difference between being on target or not. I wouldn't say I began laxative abuse in a rather bulimicy way, but I took quite a few while attending Weight Watchers and if I hadn't found the stomach cramps that went with this sort of ridiculous behaviour such agony I might have continued. Luckily I didn't. I met my target weight and left Weight Watchers behind me for ever.

I find I haven't missed the 'camaraderie' of the classes. The classes weren't compulsory; you could simply go home after the weigh-in. I usually did, but once or twice I stayed for a class. One class I remember included a weights and measures lesson. We were to guess what two ounces (that would be fifty grams to you) of ham looked like at a glance. Our leader held up a slice of supermarket 'plastic' ham and asked us to identify whether two ounces (the allowed portion measurement) was a full slice or half a slice. Of course, it was just the half slice; we all knew that, but what were you supposed to do with the other half? Put it back in the fridge of course! The reality, as we all knew, was to put one half on your plate and while you were preparing your salad the other half would magically disappear into your mouth; correct portion size maintained. Another class I stayed for was post discovering I'd put on a pound at the weigh-in. Our leader announced to all present that I needed some 'support' because I'd 'put on'. I smiled at all the sympathetic glances that came my way and left the class and never went to one again.

A note on dieting – I've mentioned the 5:2 Fast Diet as being my friend and it has been; I dropped two sizes over an eighteen-month period and the weight has stayed off, but I see it more as a lifestyle than as a diet. Back when we were cavemen we didn't bag a mammoth to feast on every day, so presumably had at least a couple of days each week munching on berries, nuts and roots – the 'fast' days. I now find it feels natural and effortless to have a 'lean' day every now and again. I call them my salad days as mostly that's what I eat on these days and as I happen to love salads they are a breeze, though I must add that the salad must be anointed with a delicious dressing as I think it's important for foods to taste good and feel satisfying and not just be good for you. I have also banned all food products labelled 'light' or 'fat free' or 'sugar free' from my larder as I believe it shouts to the Universe the message 'I think I'm fat', which I suspect the Universe then feels obliged to confirm.

So this lifestyle just makes sense to me; it suits me and my body. I have privately named this the 'Kate:Nigella Principle'. Since my stint on the 5:2 regimen I now eat this way without paying it much attention. The leaner days are the Kate Moss '*nothing tastes as good as skinny feels*' days but without the vodka and fags. Actually the skinny quote doesn't really apply but I do feel 'light' on these days and it feels good. The more indulgent days (usually at weekends) I put my Nigella Lawson hat on: '*you cannot truly say you live well unless you eat well*'. Two very beautiful, very different women whom I admire. Mostly, I aim to simply eat and drink mindfully, tune in to what my body wants and needs and aim for a peaceful relationship between my body and the fuel it requires. I did have a phase in 5:2 days when I got a bit stuck in a sort of starve/binge cycle, obsessively weighing myself and logging every morsel of food munched and every drink imbibed on MyFitnessPal app, it wasn't much fun.

As your mother I would have wanted you to see food as your fuel and your friend, not your enemy. I would have helped you all nurture a healthy body image, and especially you Lily, as it is clearly mainly women who are affected most by negatives in this department. I can't bear to see women at war with food, as so many are, and in the young, it is especially dispiriting.

My key piece of advice to you on eating would be this: 'be kind to your bodies'. It is not being kind to yourself to eat a tasteless, undressed, green salad. Neither is it kind to your body to suck down a whole bottle of Prosecco followed by a bag of salted almonds and an entire bar of Green & Black's Thin Salted Caramel Milk Chocolate (as I did last night, in fact), so I should probably add an addendum to this recommendation and that is: to 'try to be kind' and 'most of the time'. Adopt an 80/20 vibe.

It's a pet hate of mine to hear talk of diets in general and in particular while dining out, or entertaining at home. I would not have tolerated it at our family meals; it's tedious. You're munching away on something delicious and someone pipes up with some diet reference or food scare or the latest news on whether it's OK to eat butter or lard or red meat or fat in general or carbohydrates at all. As I write this letter the present 'enemy' is sugar, which at least gives fat a day off, though for sure its turn will come around again. Just as annoying is a remark that goes something like this: 'I've been good today, so I can have some pud'; i.e. I licked a lettuce leaf two days ago, had two gasps of air for lunch and as a result I am starving and desperate. I want to say to them, 'You don't have to justify it! Just enjoy your food, stop feeling guilty and savour every mouthful.'

'... I do think that women who spend all their lives on a diet probably have a miserable sex life: if your body is the enemy, how can you relax and take pleasure? Everything is about control, rather than relaxing, about holding everything in.' Nigella Lawson

—⋙⋘—

Talking of sex…back to my quest to conceive you. It was actually another five months before we had a shot at GIFT. My journals at the time were sporadic so I can't recall the reason for the delay. I have noted one or two very long cycles, which quite possibly were followed by a Tuesday or Wednesday period start date, which would have meant the treatment option wasn't on. Whatever, while the run up to the actual procedure is the same as IVF, it was much more difficult for me this time. I had to take the dreaded Buserelin nasal spray for a total of five weeks (five times a day) not the originally prescribed three and I had many more injections and scans than the first time. My response to the drugs was much more sluggish than previously, so I was required to have a higher dosage than usual. This resulted in my producing too many follicles, all likely to mature at different times. Collection of *all* of my eggs was therefore likely to be problematic and to then replace the eggs with loose sperm could result in a multiple pregnancy, which was obviously best avoided. This meant that GIFT was not an option after all and we were to go for IVF again.

This time the IVF nurse was particularly kind and caring. She suggested to me to keep thinking positive thoughts, it apparently really did increase the chances of it working. I took that on board big style and spent the next few days visualising you, as your little embryo self, making yourself at home in my womb. Dom joined me on this positive vibes theme, regularly patting my tummy and asking after 'Embers' the embryo. I found socialising particularly difficult during this waiting time. Sipping from a glass of mineral water among friends used to a person on great terms with alcohol needed an explanation. I wasn't pregnant so why was I on the wagon? I'd talked to my close girlfriends about the IVF, but I couldn't always be sure they'd told their partners. It was just plain awkward.

Members of close family knew about it, too, but again it was uncomfortable. I remember a particular family dinner out with my in-laws where I was busy supping from my large tumbler of water. I did throw in a casual reference to my status, an 'if I'm pregnant...' remark, but it wasn't acknowledged. There were no 'good lucks' or 'here's hoping' toasts, there was just a 'pregnant pause' (couldn't resist that ha!). With hindsight I realise there may have been another dimension for my husband's family to deal with. They are devout Catholics and as I have learned since the Catholic faith deems IVF as morally wrong. While not a Catholic I had married in a Catholic church and Dom's faith was important to him although he had lapsed as a practising Catholic. I'm pretty sure he was ignorant of the Catholic viewpoint on IVF; certainly he never said anything to me. As I am a non-Catholic it possibly gave him a get-out clause anyway, but it may have caused his parents some consternation, though I sincerely do hope not. Whether that was the problem or not, I certainly do *not* blame them for their awkwardness that evening. They just didn't know what to say, or how to deal with it. That's just how it is with any taboo, we simply don't have the language to discuss it and so it perpetuates. Whatever the views and behaviour of others around me, I now feel I should have just carried on as normal at this stage, had a glass of wine and switched off from it. It would have felt more natural, but knowing that there was a chance I might be pregnant meant I needed to give you the best possible start in life.

The positive feelings started to flag. It was hard work trying to keep believing when desperation was beginning to seep into my bones. The fear of having to deal with yet another disappointment started to overwhelm me. I began to wonder if it was all worth it. The stress of it all was wearing me out.

As the 'due' date grew nearer my breasts became tender and I felt nauseous; cruelly, signs of either outcome. This time I had to use some progesterone pessaries to support the embryos. Progesterone is one of the hormones necessary for maintenance of a pregnancy. On day ten post putting back the embryos I had a slight 'show'. I convinced myself it didn't necessarily indicate failure; it could be what they called 'breakthrough bleeding', couldn't it? As I write this I realise how desperate that sounds, to still cling to hope when all the signs are indicating the opposite. Once I'd completed the course of progesterone it seemed to bring on my period, so that was that. Failed again. Crushed again.

Post the failure I wanted to crawl away and hide. I didn't feel ready to bounce back and pretend everything was all right. I think I probably did though. I was often falsely cheerful and optimistic when inside I was dying. It was not a helpful practice. I had every right to feel low, but I felt it was best not to show it. 'Mrs Compliant' had become 'Mrs Stoic'. Neither role suited me. Of course, no one had died, no one was even ill, but it was as though my infertility treatment had put me out of balance with myself and with the rest of the world. I felt I had nothing to look forward to and this practice of making light of my situation felt like I was mocking it. It diminished the experience.

So, the rollercoaster had thrown me off again but I got back on, there seemed no other choice and things did get better.

Let's have a quote and I'll tell you all about 'The Good Gynaecologist'.

'He is the best physician who is the most ingenious inspirer of hope.'
Samuel Taylor Coleridge

So, there were to be no photos of you or a thank-you card from me added to the wall of the Portland fertility unit. I was reluctant to go through another IVF attempt for many reasons but mainly because I was keen to pursue another option. Back in December 1991, when Mr Pink was still treating me, I'd read an article in a fertility charity magazine by a Mr N A Armar, Consultant Obstetrician and Gynaecologist. It was about a new treatment for PCOS sufferers. The treatment was called laparoscopic ovarian diathermy, also known as ovarian drilling. It's basically a laparoscopy with add-ons: the addition of a little zapping of the ovaries with an electrically-charged needle. Quite how it works I've no idea but a few singes to each ovary somehow prompts ovulation and it was proving a successful treatment for women like me. It was never meant to be a *cure* for PCOS but a temporary repair of sorts that usually lasted long enough for a pregnancy to be achieved. In fact, around 80 per cent of women treated had become pregnant – little wonder that I was keen to find out if it could work for me. I had spoken to my GP about it at the time and she'd discussed it with Mr Pink, but he'd dismissed it as an option for me since it was aimed at patients who hadn't responded to drug treatments and I had. Technically he was right, but my response to the drugs had at times been sluggish, so I felt it was worth further investigation.

I booked a private appointment with Mr Armar at the Cromwell hospital in London almost immediately after the second IVF failure in August 1993. It was the best way of coping with the lows, to move on and do something positive. I think that's why I thought of fertility treatment as a treadmill. At times it felt relentless, like there was no respite from it, because even if I wasn't having treatment I'd either be looking for signs of ovulation or following that, the dreaded signs of menstruation. It was like being carried along on a conveyer belt that if I got off, I would then be without hope of ever reaching my destination; you, so I just kept going.

I came away from my first appointment with Mr Armar feeling more positive and optimistic about my future treatment than

I had thought possible. My only regret was that I hadn't contacted him earlier. Mr Armar was a tall, handsome and elegant man and to me looked like African royalty. He was that perfect blend of the knowledgeable, technically proficient and altruistic doctor every patient seeks but rarely finds. The sort of gynaecologist every woman deserves. He was a compassionate, patient professional who would call me by my first name and ask after Dom at each consultation (when you're married to a Super Sperm they don't have to tag along to too many appointments). Mr Armar would write down notes for himself and for me (and yes I could read his writing). He wrote with an elegant fountain pen and would draw me diagrams to explain the treatment. He gave clear, jargon-free explanations and would make detailed plans and dates for the various tests and procedures I was to undergo. Each consultation was followed by a letter reiterating what had been discussed with further clear explanations of the detail and he would often call me at home in the evening to let me know results of various tests personally. By the time of my first appointment with Mr Armar we had been 'trying for a baby' for almost five years and I had become truly desperate to have you in my life. With Mr Armar it felt like we were working together to solve the problem. He was on our side and it felt good. My time in the care of Mr Armar was shorter than that of any of the other gynaecologists who treated me but his professionalism made a lasting impact on me. Prior to Mr Armar, I had, at best, been treated as a set of ovaries and a uterus and, at worst, like a small child. Mr Armar treated Dom and me as two grown-up people with a problem. A problem that he would do his best to help us overcome.

A number of investigations had to be carried out to see if I was eligible for the ovarian diathermy. It seemed that while I clinically had polycystic ovaries, the hormone results were not typical – eventually, after more blood tests and scans I was deemed a suitable candidate for the operation and admitted to the Private

Patients Wing of University College Hospital for my zapping on 9 November 1993 (my husband's company healthcare policy kindly stumped up the cash again). It was a day-case procedure luckily and my only complaint about my treatment at UCH was the hospital porter. He delivered me back to my bed as if tipping me from a wheelbarrow. I was wearing an all-too-skimpy hospital gown and was trying desperately in my partially anaesthetised state to cover my naked backside while the transfer from trolley to bed took place. It's a small point and, of course, I appreciate that mine probably wasn't the first bare arse the porter had seen that day, he no doubt paid little attention to it, but maintaining one's dignity at these times is important. Although I have to admit the words dignity and gynaecology rarely belong in the same sentence.

Mr Armar had also said that while he was zapping the ovaries (not his term) he'd check out one or two other things. Apparently he had gleaned from my medical notes that there had been a report on a change to my womb lining in March 1992, something that I had been unaware of. Mr Armar deemed it 'important and worthy of attention'; glad someone did. So an endometrial biopsy was done and while he was about it my fallopian tubes were checked out as well. A couple of weeks later Mr Armar wrote to me saying that the procedure had gone well, my tubes were fine with very little superficial scarring from endometriosis – I didn't know I had any endometriosis. Endometriosis is a condition where the lining of the uterus grows not only inside the uterus but also in the abdomen and sometimes it can lead to scarring of the tubes or adhesions and when severe, can cause infertility. Mr Armar said I wasn't to worry, but I did apparently have widespread endometriosis in my Pouch of Douglas. What the hell is one of those? I didn't know I had one, where it was or why it was named after a chap called Douglas. I meant to ask Mr Armar but it slipped my mind; I'm sure if I had, he would have drawn me a diagram. I have since looked it up on the net and learned that the Pouch of Douglas is the space behind the womb and in front of the rectum. I also learned that endometriosis here can often cause deep pain and painful intercourse – glad to say not in my case.

All I had to do after the ovarian diathermy was to have a few more blood tests and scans to check out the hormone levels and, most importantly, whether I was now ovulating naturally. By the end of November 1993 things were looking good. I'd had my first *natural* ovulation for years. I was ecstatic! It had worked! I had a letter from Mr Armar saying that the pattern of my temperature charts was excellent and that he was sure that my husband and I would be successful in the near future if we used the relevant time in my cycle appropriately! (his exclamation mark).

There was a problem though. A problem that even dear Mr Armar, the patron saint of gynaecology, couldn't solve.

Time for a proverb!

'Desperate maladies require desperate remedies.' French proverb

During my treatment days, I did look at the alternative remedies that were available for infertility. They were less fashionable then and more difficult to get hold of, but some were beginning to emerge. I bought books on the subject as is my default strategy for anything new, difficult or otherwise in my life. For sure if I hadn't fallen at the hurdle of achieving motherhood I would have had bookshelves sagging under the weight of advice on pregnancy and child rearing, though I guess with the latter not so much time in which to read them.

The first book I purchased was a volume on aromatherapy, which I fell upon simply because it had the words 'polycystic ovary syndrome' in the index. I hoofed it down to Culpeper's in Covent Garden and bought an expensive wooden box that contained a basic selection of essential oils. I added some carrier oils, mixing bottles and the oils required for the PCOS remedy. Following the instructions I mixed a 'synergistic' blend of clary sage, fennel, geranium and rose, and massaged the oil over my abdomen every day. I wasn't convinced I'd got the blend right because I hadn't been able to get a *pure* rose essential oil; it was horrendously expensive and almost impossible to find; however, hopes were high. I wanted instant results (of course) and I'm not sure how long I kept up the daily massage of my abdomen but not long enough for a cure, obviously. However, I embraced the idea of aromatherapy; it felt like a salve to counter all the drug treatments I'd had. I booked in at my local beauty salon for an aromatherapy massage. The therapist (with whom I'd shared my infertility concerns) commented on the tension in my body. I think it was because I was so strenuously *willing* the treatment to sort out my ovaries that I was as taut as a bowstring and so it was hard to reap any real benefit, other than smelling nice afterwards.

I was introduced to an organisation called Foresight (The Association for the Promotion of Preconceptual Care); they state their role thus:

'to promote the importance of good health and nutritional status in both parents before conceiving a baby, and to provide sensible, achievable information and advice on how to do this'.

I bought their book entitled *Planning for a Healthy Baby*. I didn't finish it. Perhaps my commitment to having you wasn't quite what it should have been as I was simply not prepared to make the sacrifices they required. A hair analysis was the first step to establish the level of minerals in the body and then a diet would be devised to remove any toxins. I was prepared to eat healthily to achieve a pregnancy (and maintain one should I have been lucky enough) but the ideas I read about in the book seemed so extreme that it would be impossible to live a normal life. Remember that this was in the late eighties/early nineties when organic food was hardly spoken of and if it was, dismissed as a hippie fad. Farmers' markets didn't exist so even if I'd turned my small town garden over to a veg patch I would have been struggling to comply with the regimen. The list of lifestyle changes was huge.

Followers of this method were to avoid white flour products (breads, buns, cakes, scones, biscuits), pasta, white rice and other refined grains, packet sweets, colour carbonated drinks and most bought jams and jellies. Even potatoes were not to be peeled – the vitamin content beneath the skin being vital. No vegetables were to be fried in reheated oil, neither could they be kept warm or reheated, again to avoid loss of the vitamin content. Needless to say alcohol was a no-no. Cigarettes were taboo quite naturally. Deodorants were out of the question, too, and air fresheners and various other toxic cleaning products. Phew, just writing that down has exhausted me!

We wanted to live as normal a life as we could, which we were finding difficult enough with all the appointments and treatments. To change our lifestyle so comprehensively seemed one step too far. I really couldn't face a diet of raw veg, brown rice with a ban on beer, wine, chips and chocolate. It seemed too difficult a road to travel. These were, however, uncomfortable thoughts. If I wanted you *so* much, it was surely a small price to pay, but it should also be noted that it was essential for *both* partners to adopt the dietary changes. It hardly seemed fair on Dom, to ask him to swap beer and curry for mineral water and pulses.

I think for those with unexplained infertility it is perhaps more of an option, for there is nothing else they can do, but I knew the cause of my infertility and via IVF had at least managed to create an embryo or two. I know that many of this organisation's clients, who have embraced their methods, now have their longed-for families and I am delighted for them – they surely deserve it. There are no statistics, as far as I know, for those who haven't had success. For me it felt like yet another way to blame myself for the failure of my body. If I'd been prepared to take all the supplements and detox my body, maybe I wouldn't be writing this to you.

I also believe there is a time when it is right to say enough is enough. When I learn of couples that have endured more than ten IVF attempts, perhaps suffered miscarriages and have then decided to endure the strict dietary regime in addition, I admire their steadfastness but part of me fears for the resulting child just a little. I can only presume and hope that once the child is born all the pain and sacrifice of the journey to get there melts away.

There is a plethora of alternative remedies available now. Supermarket shelves are awash with organic foods, beauty and hygiene products and there are many more alternative treatments available. For those who remain childless it must be increasingly difficult to know when to give up the 'trying'.

I didn't need to go down the raw vegetables, no booze route, for I had Mr Armar. I think those people who eventually make the decision to give up treatment show enormous courage. I never had to make that decision, circumstances made it for me.

I think differently now about alternative ways of dealing with illness or symptoms. I am fascinated by how our emotions and thoughts can affect us physically. For sure I would have looked for the deeper meaning of any ailments you children might have presented with. If you'd developed a bad cough, for example, I might question (subtly I would hope) what was causing you to feel so irritated, as coughing can be about attempting to clear an irritant from the system, or maybe feeling guilty or shamed about something you have said or something you need to express. If the cough was keeping you awake at night I would also have bolstered up your pillows and sprayed lavender oil on your sheets to aid peaceful sleep.[6]

I have said that I think my grandmother's early death had an effect on me and I think if I was on the treatment trail now I would be aware that I was trying to make my body do something it didn't want to do, or wasn't ready to do. I fought against it, I battled my defunct ovaries and punished myself for the failures. I was at war with my body and with hindsight it was not a place where a life could begin. My body and my mind were not in harmony. With what I know now, I would have explored why I was blocking having you. It feels positive and proactive to at least try to understand what might be buried within me that was presenting itself physically as infertility.

Now I would advise anyone in this situation or any distressing scenario, to simply be kind to themself. I'm not sure I would have listened to anyone who didn't end up with a baby when I was obsessively 'trying', so I won't preach an 'I'm childless and I'm fine' sermon, but I would strongly suggest to anyone on this

---

[6] Quick tip: if you are having a sleepless night, flip your pillow over; the coolness of the other side makes it feel like you're starting the whole night again. Though as an extremely light sleeper I have some nights when I pillow flip a multitude of times and the effect does tend to wear off.

quest to fill the time away from the treatment rooms with good things, with fun and laughter, and to be gentle with yourself and your partner and, most of all, to be careful to look after your relationship. To look after each other.

I think Dom and I did try to do that during our time on the treatment treadmill. Post the first IVF failure we booked a holiday to the Caribbean and had a wonderful relaxing time. We also took a couple of trips to New York and spent time in France and Italy holidaying with friends. All of these were wonderful distractions and gave us relief from the cycle of hope and despair. We were *trying* to live normal lives but I think that we simply didn't share enough of how the whole business was affecting us. I wrote my feelings down in journals, I should have talked to my husband as well. More importantly, I should have encouraged Dom to tell me how it was for him. Hindsight is a wonderful thing.

'There is no despair so absolute as that which comes with first great sorrow, when we have not yet known what it is to have suffered and be healed, to have despaired and have recovered hope.' George Eliot, Adam Bede

As I said earlier, as a result of dear Mr Armar's skilful intervention I managed a natural ovulation – hurrah! But the euphoria was short-lived. I hit prime baby-making time and what happened? I couldn't get Dom interested in having sex with me. After all the less than spontaneous bonks at six in the morning we'd now got the chance to make a baby naturally and he couldn't be tempted. I couldn't believe it. I remember joking with a friend about it. I was casual, flippant even, but all the time I was aware of a change in him. Doubts and fears flickered across my mind. I chose to ignore them. I buried them very deeply. I had one focus. Our baby. You. It was the only thought in my head. I just wasn't prepared to contemplate the reasons why he was holding back.

I got my wish. We did manage to have sex at the appropriate time in my cycle, but sometimes you should be careful what you wish for. It wasn't good. Afterwards I felt sickened and confused. It was something of a shock too. I didn't feel violated exactly but it felt like a kind of abuse. The experience had left me feeling empty and humiliated. I remember aching to be soothed and comforted, but for the first time in my marriage I had no one to turn to.

To be honest our lovemaking had rarely set the world alight but it had always been gentle and loving. It lacked the passion of our early days but surely that was something most couples went through? We had been together nearly eight years; it was bound to become a little routine. Routine or not it had always been tender; always. Hadn't it?

On this occasion it was clearly something to be endured as far as Dom was concerned. It was the expression on his face that disturbed me the most. What was it? Revulsion? Not quite, but close enough. As he'd laboured towards his climax, it was as though someone was holding a gun to his head. He'd looked like a young, attractive gigolo servicing the tired old body of his rich and much older employer. The memory of it sickens me. I feel uncomfortable telling you this but it's my story and to leave it out would be dishonest.

I wondered what was going on in his head. What was he thinking? At the time I was too afraid to ask what was wrong. Instead, I focused on what might be a happy outcome. I muttered something about the fact that through all the good times we'd had, it hadn't worked and maybe this time it had. He didn't reply. Instead, we both lay there in a thick fug of unspoken thoughts. The atmosphere was suffocating.

I regretted pressing him for sex. My husband, it seemed, was repulsed by the very act of making love to me. I doubted that something as precious, as wonderful and as joyful as a child could come from the act we'd just performed. It was as though he had just ejaculated acid inside me. But I hung on to the idea that maybe, just maybe, all it took was a bit of bad sex to bring you into the world.

I wasn't comfortable with the idea, but after all, I'd been to a lot of trouble. Three surgical procedures in one year and all the treatments prior to that, the accompanying rollercoaster of hopes raised and then promptly dashed, had made me a desperate woman and now on top of all this my husband was a stranger to me. I loved my husband. I loved him very much and I wanted to have his children; I wanted you.

Of course, I should have talked to him about it. I should have asked him what was going on inside his head. I knew that things hadn't been good between us for a while but we weren't good communicators. We both hated conflict and disharmony and so much of the time ignored the mounting tension. We'd been in our new home just over six months and were in the process of tearing it apart. We were living in a virtual building site. We were without a proper functioning kitchen. Floorboards were up throughout the house while a new central heating system was being fitted. You could almost taste the plaster dust that hung in the air from walls being knocked through. At one point we were almost confined to one room. Add to that the stress of being on the fertility treatment treadmill and perhaps it was no wonder we found ourselves in a dark place. Dom was working longer and longer hours and I had become more isolated and desperate. I learned later that there was in, fact, another reason for all those tardy evenings in 'the office'. But whether he was at work or play, it had to be better than time spent with me: the baby obsessive. Whatever, it did us no good. It made me feel neglected and lonely, and instead of giving him a warm welcome home each evening, I'd attack him about the late hour. As a result he'd come home later and later. Various excuses were given, leaving dos (there were a lot of them), client dinners, interviewing new staff (I hoped they'd been warned about the long hours). We rowed about the hours and fell out over the work on the house and what it was costing. When we weren't arguing we sat in ugly sulky silences. Despite this I still thought it was just a bad patch. We'd had work going on in previous homes and weathered the disruption. His demanding job had been a source of conflict before and we'd got over it. Previously I'd accepted that it wouldn't be for ever and that it was a small price to pay for the high standard of living it afforded us; I could do so again. This time, however, was to be different.

On New Year's Day 1994, my husband told me that he didn't feel our relationship was right for children. He said he feared that he wouldn't be a good father, that he'd be able to provide all the material stuff but that he wouldn't be able to give enough of his time, a valid point in view of the recent rows about his working hours. I put it down to last minute jitters, like a nervous groom, he was an edgy 'father to be', but there was more to it than that.

It was difficult to hear this news without feeling truly let down. Just over a month prior I'd been given the green light from Mr Armar. All was well with my ovaries and here was my husband worried about not being able to attend your sports day! It was as if I'd just completed a marathon (and make that the same one as the guy in the antique diving suit) only to find that just as I'd crossed the finishing line I'd been disqualified. Had he been thinking this when I was being operated on just six weeks earlier? He struggled to explain to me how he felt. I suppose he dared not tell me the truth. I on the other hand am a very good talker. I am also very practised at finishing other people's sentences, so talking about it wasn't getting us very far. Shortly after his announcement we went up to Manchester to stay for a weekend with his brother and his sister-in-law and to attend the Manchester City versus Ipswich Town fixture at City's old ground Maine Road. I sat alone in the visitors' stand to support my team as, of course, I didn't want to watch the game with a load of City fans even though I was still just about married to one. We lost 4–2. I was feeling defeated in more ways than one and said to Dom after the match, 'Is that our marriage? A 4–2 win to you.' It certainly felt like it.

We arranged to see a marriage guidance counsellor. She was called Annie and I warmed to her immediately. She had kind eyes and a gentle soothing voice with an Irish lilt. She suggested at our very first meeting that we'd become too focused on bringing a baby into the world and had failed to nurture our relationship. We had simply forgotten how to have fun. All very understandable she said, but it was time for us to refocus on our relationship. It sounded a simple thing to do. Have fun again. It also crossed my mind that I should have pressed for the counselling option when having IVF at the Portland. Would I have been warned that our relationship was heading for trouble? Even given that scenario I'm not sure I'd have heeded the warning. I had thought that any problems between Dom and I were *because* we couldn't have a baby, *because* we were locked in this struggle to have you. I thought if we could take away the pain of the constant disappointments; the regular examinations, being pumped full of hormones, and the surgical procedures, all would be well in our world. I was, of course, aware that the arrival of a child changes everything and not always for the better, but I had thought our relationship to have been strengthened by surviving the ups and downs of fertility treatments, not, as was becoming clear, burned out by them.

I found the marriage guidance counselling very helpful. We went to some sessions together and some individually. In dark times I think it's fairly common to hear what you want to hear and subconsciously shut out the rest. Annie helped me hear the bad stuff. I came to trust her with my most intimate thoughts and relied upon her for insights as to why my marriage had reached this point of crisis. I learned a lot about myself and had a clearer picture of how we had come to this scenario and how we might overcome it. I wasn't sure that Dom was in the same place as me. I felt he might be attending the sessions because he felt he ought to. At home we were living with a tension of a different kind. I felt as if I had to pass some kind of test, but it seemed all the things I used to do and say – all the things he loved about me – I was no longer able to do. I tried to be cheerful and upbeat, but it seemed to aggravate him. At times I felt he loathed my very presence. I felt ugly, dull, pathetic and clingy. I was trying so hard to please him and always getting it wrong. I didn't know how to behave. I wanted to feel close to him but any approach felt awkward and he seemed to resent my attentions. The atmosphere became almost unbearable. He didn't appear to want to put things right. It all seemed like too much of an effort.

I am ashamed to admit I didn't switch off the baby button immediately. I still had the pictures of you in my head and they were vivid. On one occasion I even tried to persuade him to make love to me. I said I wasn't ovulating, when God forgive me, I was. He refused me and appalled at my behaviour I later admitted that I'd lied to him. As I write this down I'm horrified to think of myself capable of such deceit. How I could have contemplated becoming pregnant when my marriage was in such obvious difficulty I can hardly explain. I was simply desperate and hoped against hope that the promise of you arriving in our world would help me keep him. I learned from a subsequent sojourn into the world of self-help volumes that this period is recognised as 'denial'. It is the next step on from 'fear' and as I began to take in my husband's true feelings I had become very frightened indeed, so denying it was happening to me was a much easier option. But by now I had realised that his New Year's Day announcement was a deviation from the truth. He should have said that our relationship wasn't right for *him*, not that it wasn't right for children.

He left the 'family home' in early February. He moved out for some 'space'. It felt like something of a relief to start with. We had had so many heavily charged conversations. There was so much emotion sloshing about, that the peace that came from his departure was quite soothing. We continued to meet at counselling sessions and occasionally for a drink. We talked on the phone sometimes too but we didn't seem to be getting anywhere. Then at one memorable counselling session he said he wouldn't be coming back to me. He wept, kept shaking his head and left the session early. Annie and I watched him from the window as he walked away, his head in his hands. 'He's not telling us something,' was all she said; she was right.

I returned home in shock. I felt paralysed and for the rest of the day, I laid on our bed only getting up to make myself cups of tea. Tea, funny that; I'd have thought I would have dived into a large vat of alcohol but good old PG was my solace. Since that day tea has been a constant companion – I drink gallons.

'There is no trouble so great or grave that cannot be much diminished by a nice cup of tea.' Bernard-Paul Heroux

I found I couldn't leave the sanctuary of our bedroom. I couldn't actually weep either; I was numb. At times I couldn't breathe. Panic attacks hit me hard. I'd wake up in the night, boiling hot and struggling for air. In this dark time I learned, not just to take a day at a time, but sometimes I'd have to break up time into more manageable increments; taking life an hour at a time or even aiming to cope with the next five minutes became my strategy to cope. It might sound extreme but at times I truly felt in despair. And all of the time I was trying to work out why.

I was to learn shortly after this that the 'space' he'd moved out for was, in fact, space in which to shag someone else. I felt doubly betrayed. While I'd been trying to find ways to rebuild our relationship he'd been busy digging foundations elsewhere.

He told me on a Sunday, six weeks after he'd moved out. He'd called and arranged to come round for a chat. I had planned a roast chicken dinner, his favourite. I greeted him at the door with a 'nice day at the office dear' sort of kiss, feeling at odds with the fact that he'd knocked on his own front door instead of letting himself in with his key. We sat down at the kitchen table, the chicken sizzling away in our new trendy stainless steel oven (the brand name we'd previously chuckled over was Siemens).

I noticed a red patch on his neck and some little raised white bumps. A nervous rash? Possibly. At least it ought to have been, because before I could say anything he announced that he was seeing someone else. His words were like a sharp blow to my stomach. I asked him if he loved her – of course. He said no. I asked him if the sex was good. He shook his head in disbelief at the question. I asked him if she was blonde with big tits. I was dark haired at the time with average sized breasts, though I'm blonde now (they have more fun apparently) plus my shade of 'menopausal blonde' suits the pallor of the old bird I am now. I certainly do not want to go down the Paul McCartney route of staying with the same hair colour of my youth; in my opinion it makes one look ghostly (and faintly ridiculous). Of course, I didn't really want to know what his new sex life was like, or anything about the appearance of the woman he was now having sex with. I was trying to be funny; no one was laughing.

Delicious roasty dinner smells filled our new bespoke kitchen, but I'd lost my appetite. Alcohol though had at last come into its own. I was drinking vodka and tonic, large ones. I asked him if he was hungry and rather shamefaced he admitted that he was starving. I produced the final Sunday roast of our marriage and begged him not to get her pregnant.

I don't need to say that this revelation turned my world upside down. I continued to go and see Annie and I listened to breakup songs. You need sad songs when you're sad. Everything But The Girl were my artists of choice during this particular time; their album *Amplified Heart* became the soundtrack of my life and on a raw day it can still move me to tears. They also penned the only song I've ever heard about longing for a child 'Apron Strings', another tear-jerker for me. I did a 'Rob Fleming' from

Nick Hornby's novel *High Fidelity* and created a cassette tape[7] of all the songs that really said how it was for me. I made a copy and gave it to Dom; he said it made him weep.

All the time I was trying to understand what had happened to us. I didn't want to hate him, I wanted to carry on loving him. I wanted to heal him, to heal us; of what or how I still wasn't sure. I just wanted to make it right.

During this time the need to have a baby barely registered; you were gone from my mind. I leaned on family and friends for love, support and comfort. I found the mood swings during this time to be totally unpredictable and extraordinary. Sometimes I could feel quite positive thinking that this was just a phase Dom was going through; that we would overcome it and be the stronger for it. At other times I would hit a pit of gloom, fearful of the future and despairing of the present. I would habitually get two mugs down from the cupboard when making tea or coffee and it stung every time. Even ordinary everyday errands felt painful; at the supermarket checkout I felt there was a neon sign above my head pointing at me saying 'meals for one'. I was still buying his favourite foods with no appetite to eat them.

I became something of a self-help junkie; returning from my local Waterstones with various volumes on relationships and how to deal with their derailment. I needed to understand what had caused my marriage to break down and what I could do about it. I found some of the guidance on how to cope a bit hard to take seriously. 'Making peace with my inner critic' and 'allowing fear to become my friend' didn't seem to offer the key to long-term happiness. I also drew the line at writing positive notes to myself

---

[7] This is a word from my 'dinosaur dictionary' and not something you will have had occasion to use. It is a plastic case the size of an iPhone that holds audio tape in which the tape passes from one reel to another when being played. I guess if you wanted to do the same you would simply make a playlist.

like 'you have a pretty smile' and sticking them to the bathroom mirror. But while I was finding a strategy to cope, I knew that the books couldn't give me the answers I wanted to hear. In fact, I knew that 'answers' weren't necessarily available to any of my questions. Annie told me at one session that I might have to accept that I would never really know 'why' my marriage had failed. I would come to know the contributing factors that had got our marriage into trouble, and I was prepared to take the blame, but I struggled to understand why it couldn't be repaired.

Later that year I joined a group for separated people called Breakthrough, which met on Monday evenings. It wasn't a social, meeting people sort of thing, but a workshop-style evening where together we would work through various exercises from a book called *Rebuilding* to help us come to terms with the breakdown of our relationships. There were ten of us; all different ages, shapes and sizes and with the exception of one person, we had all been dumped. We were the 'dump*ees*'. The one person attending who had done the dumping was a slight timid little woman who didn't last the course. I wasn't surprised; there was such an instant bond between those of us that had been rejected. We were all from different backgrounds, some married for twenty-five years, some for just two, some with children and me and one other chap without. A disparate group linked by one thing in common: whatever our differing circumstances we recognised in each other a shared experience which rendered our differences an irrelevance. Some of us were further down the line than others; some were very raw. It had been six months since the last roast dinner of my marriage and with the help of Annie, family, friends and an excess of relationshipy books, I was getting by. There were often tears from some people in the group (not from me, I'm not one for public displays of emotion) but when a member broke down it was never a problem, it wasn't difficult or embarrassing, just part of the process.

I remember one particular evening when we were working on 'Self-worth'. For our 'homework' we'd had to prepare a list of ten things we liked about ourselves. Sadly, an extremely difficult thing to do; so much easier to come up with ten things wrong with you. Most people hadn't bothered but me the self-help junkie and another woman I'd had a lot of telephone contact with had. We read ours out to lots of nods and mumbles of approval – I don't need to tell you how excruciating it was. Afterwards we were each given a little pad of paper where we were required to write 'I like (blank) because' and proceed to list positive things about our fellow group members. We were to do this for each person while they sat on their hands and squirmed with embarrassment. I recall one woman's turn and I couldn't think of a single thing to write about her. Nightmare. Obviously, I couldn't sit chewing the end of my pen, brow furrowed looking stumped for inspiration, so I hastily wrote down something about shiny hair and a nice smile, which wasn't strictly true, and then I added something about courage, which was.

When I received my little sheaf of notes, it was clear that my earlier reading of the list I had compiled had helped, because many people had simply reiterated what I had said about myself. Nevertheless I was curiously pleased with my 'I like Tess because…' notes and more than twenty years on I still have those little bits of paper. Worth remembering, I think, that when a good thing is written down, it becomes a gift that keeps on giving.

What I learned from all this 'self-discovery' was that my priorities had been turned on their head. I was no longer grieving for the inability to have my own biological child; to have you. I was grieving for the loss of my partner. It felt like a loss so huge I wasn't sure I could endure it. The pain of childlessness was upstaged by a deeper pain. As with the grief of childlessness there was no actual death, no funeral to go to, no official goodbye. This was made worse (or better as it seemed to me at the time) by the fact that the door back to my husband was always left ajar.

'…a broken heart mends much faster from a conclusive blow than it does from slow strangulation.' Diana Athill

Often when I met up with him or spoke to him on the phone he seemed confused and upset. I think he wanted to let me down gently but unfortunately it just meant I kept hanging on. I would visit the local Catholic church in Kew, a beautiful little church and a place of hope for me. I would light candles, tears rolling down my cheeks, on my knees, praying for his return to my life. All the while plumbers, electricians and carpenters continued to ransack our home.

I moved away from the imagined moments with you my children and into another fantasy life of daydreaming about reconciliation and a new, better life together. I would regularly go for walks around my beloved Kew Gardens. I would walk around the less populated perimeter of the gardens away from the crowds of visitors with pictures in my head of warm encounters with Dom, of starting a new life abroad with him. I would rehearse getting back together, 'I still love you' conversations with him. He had talked of working in Hong Kong and I imagined visiting him there, emerging blinking from the flight, feeling the heat of the strange foreign air and the joy of recognising love in his eyes. I would visualise my own version of the scene from *Sleepless in Seattle* (actually a reference to the classic movie *An Affair to Remember*) where the 'should be together' lovers meet atop the Empire State Building. Whatever the scenario, however far-fetched, I would let my mind transport me to a heavenly place where we were together again and more deeply in love; healed. These thoughts gave me a peace I couldn't find any other way. I had spent years loving this man and yearning to bear his children; dreaming of you; us, our family. I simply could not let go. All of a sudden the life I had worked so hard to build, that of wife and mother, was no longer available to me. I analysed his every word, his every gesture, even his silences to the point of exhaustion. When I wasn't daydreaming, facing reality was like having a huge ulcer in my mouth, which my foolish tongue would not stop seeking out, like an irresistible urge to feel and re-feel the pain.

'I like living. I have sometimes been wildly, despairingly, acutely miserable, racked with sorrow, but through it all I still know quite certainly that just to be alive is a grand thing.' Agatha Christie

I was to spend the following two years coming to terms with this huge change, and throughout that time I always thought I would still end up with you, my family. My estranged husband and I were learning more about each other during these months apart than we ever had in all our time together. It seemed a waste not to build on this greater knowledge. We had at last learned to communicate, but it seemed it was just to negotiate our final farewells.

I don't regret all the daydreaming and 'wasted' hours fantasising about reconciliation. It was simply my way of dealing with it; and life in general. During this time I compiled a list of things to do when feeling at a low ebb and I still practise many of these things now. Walking is most certainly the greatest salve. Whatever the problem, I have found that I *always* feel better about it after a walk.

'Solvitur ambulando… It is solved by walking…' St Augustine

I don't just walk when I'm sad; it helps me mull things over generally. I walk daily and wouldn't be without it. Another thing on my go-to list when feeling down is to make myself look pretty (within reason). Bouffing up my hair and applying a little make-up makes me look better and therefore I feel better. A kitchen bop to an old favourite can lift me, or a flick through my scrapbooks[8] can distract me and shift my mood to a better place.

Sometimes though, the time is right to have a bit of a wallow in the trough of pain. There is a strange comfort in deep sorrow.

'The human heart dares not stay away too long from that which hurt it most. There is a return journey to anguish that few of us are released from making.' Lillian Smith

Giving in to it could be dismissed as succumbing to self-pity but it's subtler than that. Enduring this painful period in my life gave me a grace I'd never had before. I made new friends and re-acquainted myself with old ones. I was kind to myself. I bought myself flowers and relaxed in heavenly scented candlelit baths. I wrote down how I felt; pages and pages of bare emotion.

When I wasn't daydreaming I was getting on with my life. To fill the empty evenings I became an evening class junkie. I signed up for a stained-glass-window-making class, and one on special paint effects in addition to my part-time day class on interior design. I later enrolled at Chelsea College of Art to study interior

---

[8] I am a 'mag hag'. I love magazines (particularly those on interiors) and I clip any pleasing images and add them to my scrapbooks, slightly anal possibly but a simple activity that gives me endless pleasure. I also do Pinterest.

design full-time. I also particularly enjoyed a course on screen-writing and wrote many a script with, not surprisingly, the main theme being relationship breakdown. At times I even began to enjoy the freedoms my new life as a singleton offered.

By October, seven months of living alone, all the work on the house had been completed and I had tastefully (in my opinion) redecorated the interior throughout. It had been hard work; I'd decorated every room (with some help from my parents), I'd made curtains, painted furniture (up-cycled as it is now called) I'd even replastered (badly) the ceiling in the utility room. The work had given me purpose and I was pleased with the result, but the 'family' home in Kew was no longer the home I wanted. I was beginning to feel properly 'single' again and while I was still pining and dreaming of a reconciliation with Dom, there was another part of me that wanted to move on and move out.

In July 1995 after I had completed the interior design course at Chelsea and eighteen months post Dom's New Year's Day proclamation, we agreed to sell the marital home and quickly received an offer for the full asking price. The massive increase in the value of the property made me feel good. The knowledge (or proof) that my work on improving the property meant that I had at least earned some income for the partnership. I wasn't just a meekly 'kept' woman (without the sex). I decided to rent a property until I determined what I wanted to do with my life. Dom generously offered to support me for a couple of years until I had built a new career. I didn't want to return to my former career of marketing and event organising and the world of interior design that I'd studied to join felt too exclusive and impossible. I was strongly feeling that I'd like to make a living from writing (even more impossible).

'Our trials, our sorrows, and our grieves develop us.'
Orison Swett Marden

Notting Hill felt like the place for wannabe scriptwriters to live so after the house was sold I rented a one bedroom flat there. While I was at times excruciatingly lonely, I found adopting the 'take each day at a time' approach to life suited me. It was a relief not to be living for some glorious day in the future when I would become your mother. At darker times it felt like I had failed at something else but I had at least learned that infertility was *not* the worst thing to happen to me. At around this time Dom told me that I had made him a better person. It's a remark that to this day I take out like a treasured old possession; shine it up, look at it for a while and smile, though…

'When two people part it is the one who is not in love who makes the tender speeches.' Marcel Proust, In Search of Lost Time

The pain of childlessness had become insignificant compared to this separation; this rejection. I was adapting though and slowly starting to recover. I was getting on with my life. But all the while I knew that if Dom were ever to look at me the way he used to and tip my chin with the base of his thumb, I would be healed. Longing for a child to love that you can't have is a huge sadness. Loving someone who no longer loves you is an unutterable sorrow.

'Someone I loved once gave me a box full of darkness. It took me years to understand that this too was a gift.' Mary Oliver

So, my journey so far meant I'd lost a husband and all hope of having you, but…

'It is astonishing how short a time it can take for very wonderful things to happen.' Frances Hodgson Burnett

When are you ready to meet someone else? I'm not sure I ever was but about nine months (interesting time span?!) after husband *numero uno* moved out for 'space' I entered something of a 'slapper' phase. I had a number of liaisons with inappropriate partners. They were either far too young for me, on a different wavelength completely or, heaven forfend, in a relationship with somebody else. It seemed being betrayed by someone I loved didn't preclude me from committing the same offence, but it was only the once and a drunken one-night-stand-style liaison, so I managed to assuage my guilt. Besides I had no intention of stealing anyone else's man since I was still frozen in a limbo, unable to let go of my estranged husband. However, one year and nine months on from the 'space' exit and almost exactly two years since Mr Armar had zapped my ovaries, I met my second husband Des, while visiting friends in Cornwall.

I was still madly hanging on to the idea of reuniting with my first husband but paradoxically feeling open towards meeting someone else. Des and I had nothing in common whatsoever (still haven't ha!) other than the fact we had both been dumped by our spouses. Another experience shared was that he too had been 'trying for a family'. It seemed both our partners had gone to try their luck elsewhere.

We had been seeing each other for around a month; me regularly making the journey from Notting Hill to Cornwall, and Christmas was fast approaching, when I found myself in the Accident and Emergency department of the Royal Cornwall Hospital in Truro.

We had been up to Suffolk for Des to meet my parents for the first time and to deliver Christmas presents. We then spent the rest of the weekend catching up with friends in London and Christmas shopping, before commencing a tortuous journey back to Cornwall in freezing fog. A journey that should normally be around four and a half hours took us ten. It was very early days in the relationship and this ridiculously long journey from where I deemed at the time to be 'civilisation', meant that doubts started to fill my mind, not about the man, but about where he lived. It was simply too far away. Too far from all I loved and valued. Too far away from all I knew. Thoughts like: 'This isn't going to work' and 'I'll give it until after Christmas' spun around in my head. I didn't share these thoughts, we were both tired and pissed off after the journey, but I felt awkward, uncomfortable and downcast after a thoroughly enjoyable weekend that should have left me feeling the opposite.

The following Monday evening, I was feeling rested and brighter but the doubts were still there and I'd pretty much decided that a life with this Cornishman wasn't for me. It seemed the Universe had other plans. That evening I slipped on a wet floor and broke my ankle. It meant I was unable to drive for seven weeks. I could have asked Des to drive me up to my parents where I could have made my recovery but it didn't occur to me. Des and his family got on with the job of looking after me. He cooked, washed, cleaned and ironed during this honeymoon phase of our relationship. He learned how to cook pasta dishes and even pretended to like them.

In the weeks following, my resistance to a life with this Cornishman melted and I made my decision to move from London to Cornwall and embrace the life of the countrywoman. I was moving on from my man in Paul Smith suits with smooth hands and pipe-cleaner arms, for a tanned, rugged countryman with rough working hands and big strong Popeye arms.

It wasn't the outcome I'd expected; but at last I felt safe and loved.

Through much of our first eighteen months together we were both, in part, grieving for our previous relationships and I was also learning to let go of my London life. My trips back to London were fairly frequent and Des would sometimes accompany me *Crocodile Dundee* style. While I shopped and bemoaned the lack of any decent shops in Cornwall (not even the essential John Lewis), he chatted to anglers in Hyde Park and introduced himself to bemused punters in my Notting Hill local. Mostly during this time we shared our experiences, our feelings and our dreams. Despite all our differences, we simply held on to one another as we both gradually let go of the past, and helped each other through our respective divorces. Hearing of the pregnancy of Dom's then girlfriend was the trigger for me to finally let go. I don't think I need to elaborate.

'Well, being divorced is like being hit by a Mack truck. If you live through it, you start looking very carefully to the right and to the left.' Jean Kerr

I went the DIY route for my divorce and as we'd already settled the financial arrangements it was straightforward. I pitched up at our local Citizens Advice and got a leaflet. After sorting out the paperwork I found myself in the bizarre situation of swearing on a bible in the offices of Cornwall County Council; the bible being pushed towards me under a glass counter not unlike passing a paying-in-book to the cashier in a bank. It did strike me at the time as being discordant with the enormity of the emotion that goes with getting divorced. It was just like getting a TV licence. People can be sniffy about divorcees. They are usually the 'smug marrieds'. The fact is I never wanted to become one and will do all I can to make sure it doesn't happen again. But as I learned from that experience it takes two and if one wants out, there is not a lot the other can do. Besides longevity is not necessarily the best measure of a successful union. The truth is many of the 'smug marrieds' busy notching up the years are often in some of the most stagnant of relationships, afraid to pack it in and get themselves a better life. People have said to me, what a bastard your first husband was for deserting you the way he did. No he isn't. He's a nice guy, of course he is, I married him. We're all here just doing our best to lead a happy life. We were great friends; our friendship I have missed as much as anything else and his family too, whom I loved very much, but shit happens. I hope he's happy with his wife and his three children. The years we had together were pretty much happy ones and I am grateful for them. So, the pearl of wisdom (?) I want to pass on to you here, is that not all good marriages last for ever and not all bad marriages end.

My transition from city sophisticate (?) into countrywoman wasn't smooth. I resisted much of the change to start with. While settling into village life I felt duplicity in longing for so much of what my previous urban existence had given me. There was a dichotomy in my feeling for my country life. I loved the welcome in the village shop; I loved being called 'beautiful' by the guy who ran the local petrol station. I still love the way the Cornish use terms of endearment randomly to strangers; to be called 'sweetheart', 'my love' and the like by shop assistants, ticket inspectors, taxi drivers is the norm in Cornwall. Though however warm my welcome to Cornish life was, I still craved the London shops and trendy bars and restaurants. I think I also missed the strange kudos that I have always felt goes with living in our capital city, the urbane quality I sought from my W11 postcode. There was no internet at this time, none of the online browsing and super-fast delivery that us country dwellers enjoy today. At home, I reminded myself of actress Penelope Keith's character Margo Leadbetter, in the seventies sitcom *The Good Life*. I was that person wearing Marigolds and cashmere to feed the chickens and I'm ashamed to say I was at times also looking down from a great height on the local yokels. Gradually though I gave in to it and fell in love with Cornwall and the tiny community I'd been welcomed into.

A few years on and we moved into our dream home. An old and very beautiful farmhouse with spectacular views on the outskirts of the village. I became a slave to the Farrow & Ball paint chart ordering an insane number of sample pots some shades so barely indistinguishable from the others it was ridiculous and once again I was starting to look like a paintbrush, decorating our new home throughout. I laboured in the overgrown garden to tame it and make it mine and also created a new vegetable garden to tend. I was in heaven. Still am.

Our farmhouse kitchen came with an Aga and while I'd been told it would be the beginning of a love affair with Aga cooking, I was sceptical. I was wrong. I did fall in love and it has made me a better cook and made entertaining more of a pleasure. Des later bought me the iconic KitchenAid mixer and that combined with my newfound love for the Aga meant I could add baking to my list of life skills. I now bake cakes for friends and family and for local fund-raising events. I would have loved to bake birthday cakes for you; big, fat, gooey chocolate ones.

I've learned many other essentially 'country' domestic skills like plucking the feathers from a game bird or goose. I will even cheerfully stick my hand up its backside and drag its guts out without a qualm. I can also gut fish and fillet them (badly). I can pick a crab, shuck an oyster, clean and prep a scallop and de-vein a lobster. So I've settled into my Cornish country life and it feels like the right life for me; it would also have been a perfect life to have brought children into. I'm sure you would have been happy here.

As to 'trying for a family' Des and I never took steps to prevent a pregnancy, but by the time I felt truly committed to my countryman and my country life I was thirty-seven and our underlying feeling was that it was too late and I was starting to imagine you in my life less and less. I was also aware that the ovarian diathermy benefits had almost certainly ceased. I wasn't sure if I was ovulating at all and didn't feel inclined to start taking my temperature again or to buy ovulation kits to see if I was. Ever since the diathermy and Dom's departure I'd experienced what I called 'peaceful periods'. Mr Armar had cured the oligomenorrhoea so my menstrual cycle was now a regular, simply physical and natural process no longer accompanied by spiralling hopes followed by despair. I knew too that some women had the magic electro-diathermy more than once, but I simply couldn't face attending Mr Armar's consulting rooms anytime soon. The move from London to rural Cornwall would have made access to treatment even more arduous and I felt too weary and possibly too afraid to try again. My eggs were dodgy at age thirty-two; I couldn't imagine that they had improved any in the passing years. Des and I decided to just let fate decide. If I had conceived you we'd have been delighted, but I had stepped out of the circle of hope and disappointment and I didn't want to go back. I couldn't face the stress and strain of any further treatment and although I was aware of the pressure the whole process places on a relationship, it was not that fear that prevented me from pursuing it. I was now in a relationship where I knew I was deeply loved and valued, and I was happy. It was enough.

Des and I have a great need to demonstrate our love for the children and young people that we do have in our lives. Des is a magnet to young children, largely I suspect because he is simply a big kid himself. I have read that many childless people retain childlike qualities; perhaps it's because our lives lack the stress of the huge responsibility that goes with being a parent. Certainly on long summer days on the beach when other women are shouting at their kids not to throw stones or to splash one another, I find myself shouting to my middle-aged husband not to do the same. Watching him entertaining children and how they respond to him can be bittersweet moments for me. I can't help but imagine how it would have been if he'd become your father when I see evidence of the dad he might have been.

'She was no longer wrestling with her grief, but could sit down with it as a lasting companion and make it a sharer in her thoughts'
George Eliot, Middlemarch

Accepting that you will never have your own biological children is a very gradual process. It's like bereavement in that it eases with time, feels less raw, but every now and then it takes you by surprise by its re-emergence. I have heard the sadness associated with childlessness referred to as 'unfocused grief'. Unfocused or not it feels like a very real grief and like the wretchedness that accompanies separation and divorce; it is a mourning for which we have no ceremony. I call it 'cloaked grief' or 'masked grief' but whatever name I label it with it doesn't feel like 'proper' grief as it lacks the ritual: the funeral, the sympathy cards and the memories to share. It is a process that is familiar and with it brings some comfort, but grieving for you, my children who never existed, grieving for a role to play that I have been denied, has no process. There is no shock or finality of a person no longer being there. There is no jarring, raw emptiness. It is simply a gradual fading of hope that becomes a slow dull ache. For some it begins when the treatment options have run out, or a decision (a brave one) has been made to give up treatment. Or, as in my case, a change of circumstances has meant that the baby quest is over.

I'm not sure how much longer I would have carried on with treatment if Dom hadn't shipped out. Since my trust and confidence in Mr Armar was so strong, I'm sure I would have been guided by him as to what the next best step might have been. Instead all I could do was write a letter to him telling him of my change in circumstance. I felt mean for mucking up his statistics. I was convinced that I could have been an addition to his 'success' rates but had to accept that I would appear as a tick in the 'no' box for pregnancy achieved. I wondered how many other of his patients had so carelessly lost their husbands during treatment.

The realisation that I would never meet you, never feel your skin against mine, never know your love for me, never sense your need for me crept up on me slowly. Quietly and softly I recognised that this was how it was going to be. In bereavement one does not want to forget the person they are grieving for and neither do

I. I don't want to just forget the loss that I feel for never having you in my life. Being childless is part of who I am and you too are a part of me.

As I am now in the land of the menopausal, where motherhood is clearly impossible, it has got easier; pregnancies and births among my contemporaries are rare. I did struggle when an acquaintance began her family at the age of forty-one (when I was forty-one) but news of 'oldies' having babies now is easier to hear. However, I am aware of times in the future when my loss might be keener felt than at present. When my friends' children get married, when they're busy choosing their hats, interfering with the seating plan and caterers; moaning about or (more hopefully) exulting their sons and daughters-in-law, I will be reminded of you: the children I never had.

When they become grandparents, I will be reminded of another role I cannot play and so it goes on. I have adapted to this life as a non-mother but I realise there are many contradictions in the way I have dealt with this aspect of my life. I don't want people to sympathise with me but to show me understanding and yet I rarely make plain my feelings to enable anyone to do so. I don't know if this is common among childless people or whether I'm uniquely tongue-tied on the subject, though my tendency to muteness is not really a surprise. At the time of the 'oldie' pregnancy that I mentioned earlier I did reach out to share my feelings. I was emailing a friend about something else and popped in a line that I was having a wobble about the late start on the road to maternity of this person we both knew. The 'wobble' was never acknowledged. I wonder why. The curse of the taboo?

Writing about my childlessness has been my solution, through my journals and by writing this letter to you.

'Write to be understood, speak to be heard, read to grow.' Lawrence Clark Powell

It's not the first letter I've written to you. I wrote to you in November 2001; it was around the time when I was struggling with the news of the 'oldie' pregnancy. The letter around two pages of A4 was a gushy missive full of love and wonder. You would only have been aged about eight, six and if I'd had a third child four. Again I wrote of the sort the mother I would have been to you then and the life we would have shared. How I would have loved you – oh how I would have loved you. I signed it 'All my love my angels, Mummy' and I put three kisses beneath. I can hardly put into words how it felt to write the word 'Mummy'; for the briefest of moments it felt real. I think that first letter heralded my acceptance. It was a cathartic exercise to express my love for you at last.

I still feel this love for you, it's deep within me, but with no-where for it to go. Sometimes when I feel a little tug of grief at having never really known you, I read the first letter I wrote to you, and yes dear children, I read it and weep.

Much of the struggle in coming to terms with childlessness stems from the reactions of other people. It's just plain embarrassing to mention kids to someone who can't have them. For us involuntarily childless peeps can be tricky to deal with. Worse though, for me, is when people have misconstrued our situation as not *wanting* children. To have endured all sorts of invasive treatments to have a child and then to be looked upon as someone who might not even *like* kids is tough. I have had a difficulty here; in the past and particularly in the 'trying years' I often didn't cuddle babies in public to avoid any random 'Tess is feeling broody'-style comments. I am aware that by avoiding holding babies I might have given a false impression. When I have held babies in the company of understanding friends I have found it a simply heavenly experience. The smell of them, the softness of their skin, their tiny perfect features, their vulnerability. Some mothers have been able to be generous to me with their children. They've made me feel trusted with their precious infants. I especially hold dear the times I have spent alone with the babies of family and friends. Some mothers have made me feel the opposite but I have always tried to understand and respect their position, as had I found myself placed in the same situation I'm not sure I would have been all that generous passing you around into the care of others.

I believe it is no coincidence that my coming to terms with my infertility has happened at that time in life when my natural fertility (had I had such a thing) would have been on the wane anyway. My contemporaries don't yearn to have a baby now and quite naturally, neither do I.

However, I still have an anxiety about my status as non-mother. There is an overriding feeling that I am something 'less than' as I can't do the one thing that only women can do: give birth. It is a sad fact but women are so often defined by their fertility.

'I am hurt, hurt and humiliated beyond endurance, seeing the wheat ripening, the fountains never ceasing to give water, the sheep bearing hundreds of lambs, the she-dogs, until it seems the whole country rises to show me its tender sleeping young while I feel two hammer blows here instead of the mouth of my child.' Federico García Lorca, Yerma

It doesn't happen very often any more, probably because I'm in my early fifties, but it's a relatively recent alteration. Some time ago, I guess I was in my late thirties, I was sitting quietly with my hubbie Des, sipping a pint in my local pub and smiling broadly at a most delightful little girl, aged around three. She was a bright little kid and simply exuded a joy for living. As her parents perused the menu board the little girl stood on a nearby chair and looked up at them. Her eyes were bright and glossy and wide open. I remember noticing a strawberry birthmark beneath her left eye and fearing she might feel self-conscious about it in later life. She announced that she would like a sandwich, added an unprompted 'please', giggled and ran back to where her grandmother was sitting, nursing a baby in her arms. Seeing the sweetness in this child and her natural capacity for joy instilled in me a peaceful, all is well in the world feeling. Then the barmaid, who had been watching me, watching the girl, promptly spoiled the moment by barking across the room 'Feeling broody Tess!' I groaned inwardly. At that time I had been feeling broody for well over a decade.

On those occasions I would normally have just let out an embarrassed laugh and brushed the remark to one side but that day I wasn't in the mood. I just muttered under my breath something about not being able to have kids. I said it in a low voice and avoided eye contact. I regretted my remark instantly. The barmaid wasn't to know my situation, so why embarrass her? I don't think I had as it goes, for she immediately drew my attention to the baby the little girl's grandmother was holding, remarking on the child's beautiful eyes. As I looked at them I found I couldn't agree, to me they looked large and bulbous, but it could have just been wind. I concurred with the barmaid anyway and diverted my attention to the menu board. It was the evening menu and sadly for the little girl, there were no sandwiches listed.

As I said earlier, this doesn't happen very often any more and I'm glad, but I still feel uncomfortable whenever there is a reference as to whether I have any children. I feel I should be more prepared by now and deal with it by way of a simple easy sentence, but I find I never am. Small talk is the danger area. For most people it's just a dull and boring prelim to getting to know someone better or before deciding that you don't want to get to know them at all. For me, small talk can become all about avoiding 'the children question'. It doesn't matter what the occasion, the wedding reception where I discover my name card is placed beside someone I've never met before, the Christmas party when I'm playing the part of corporate wifey or simply at a function when I find myself chatting to someone I don't know very well. The small talk begins, pleasantries are exchanged and I can sense the enquiry coming my way. I begin to tense and start feeling uptight and then out pops the question that so often I find myself ill-equipped to answer.

'Have you got any children?'

The person making this enquiry cannot possibly imagine the impact it has on me, and why should they? It is after all a question that should be easy to reply to, a simple yes or no, surely? An answer 'Yes' would be easy. It would invariably lead to the disclosure of more information; ages, names and so on, quickly and easily divulged. The facts freely given and a pleasure to share.

I struggle with my answer, for it is not a pleasure to share. I can hardly say: 'Yes, I have a daughter Lily and a son and possibly a third, but they're imagined, not real.' The problem is a 'No' also seems to require further explanation and all too often I have found myself unable to provide it. Sometimes I just say, 'No' and look wistful, or I say, 'Sadly no', again adding a bit of wistful. I guess the wistful stuff is to try to prompt an acknowledgement of my situation. I have rarely got it. People just shrug and very often look embarrassed, as if they've accidentally discovered a rather dirty secret. Without fail I always wish I'd handled it better. I have tried the direct and honest approach and once when asked by an acquaintance as to why we didn't have kids, I barked, 'I'm

INFERTILE that's why' and watched the poor man inwardly shrink and crawl away. I felt mean, sorry for embarrassing him and I have never answered the question in that way again since. I have been known to be glib about it and say the opposite of how I'm feeling. I once trotted out this remark, 'I've got better things to do with my time.' I could hardly believe my own ears. Why on earth had I said that?

So why do I struggle to answer the question? Am I embarrassed? Yes, I suppose so. I am also just a little ashamed. It is, for me, an admission of failure. At times being asked if I have kids simply reaffirms my sense of loss. A sense of loss that I have rarely been able to share. When people are grieving or are sad that a relationship has ended, or unhappy for any other reason, it is accepted that there will be a need to share the experience. At these times people are drawn to fellow sufferers, those who can truly empathise with how it feels. The truth is that until recently I have dealt with the pain of childlessness largely by pretending that I'm not that bothered. I'm not sure how to advise you here; I'm not suggesting you never ask the question, but perhaps simply try to be more creative in small talk situations if you can.

The trouble with infertility is the taboo. I don't even know if any of the childless couples in my social circle feel the same way as I do. There aren't many of them; almost all of my close friends have a family. Those without may have decided against having children and think of themselves as child*free*, not child*less* and are therefore not grieving for the lack of their own children. I know one of them most certainly is, but do we ever talk about it? Almost never. My older brother doesn't have children of his own, we've briefly touched upon the subject and I think he's fine with it but I can't honestly say for sure. Through no fault of our own we cannot belong to a club that almost all of our close friends and family are members of and yet strangely we never discuss this situation with each other.

I feel that involuntary childlessness will become less of an unmentionable due to the fact that more women are deferring having families until later in their lives (when their fertility is on the wane) so a childless life will be a more common outcome. However, these women won't necessarily garner more sympathy, as most likely a 'serves them right for leaving it too late' response to their dilemma will be fired at them – sorry, that sounded negative.

Apple and Facebook recently announced that they will provide a benefit package to include freezing the eggs of their young female employees. I was taken aback. These women would be embarking on the same sort of treatment programme that the infertile endure. Freezing eggs is, of course, an understandable road to travel for a woman facing a medically indicated need such as cancer, but as a deferment for a healthy young woman so she can 'have it all' seems a risky endeavour. I fear that using it as some sort of safeguard for career and baby-making options is foolhardy. It also seems glib and inappropriate to plan for a child when it's simply convenient, like making an extra lasagne to bung in the freezer at the weekend to save the hassle of cooking mid-week after a hard day at work.

When I hear discussions in the media or in general (and there are a lot of them) about women 'juggling' their lives to have a family and a career I often feel that my childlessness has made me a bad feminist. To hear women bemoaning the dent in their careers that child rearing is going to inevitably mean, feels such a negative outlook to me. To focus on the collateral damage to a career that bringing a brand new human being into the world causes seems disingenuous. Of course, maternity leave means a lot of sick, shit, sore nipples and crushing fatigue but there is surely a wee bit of joy to be enjoyed as well. If I'd had a career that I loved and I'd been able to have you as well, I'd have hoped that I might have focused on getting a balance in my life, and if my career had lost its glint as a result of your arrival, I would have hoped that the sheer wonder of your existence might have enriched my life sufficiently to more than make up for that loss.

I'm going to sound very Pollyanna'ish here, but I like to look for the good whenever I can and I believe a lot of women waste energy looking for inequality. I'd rather focus on how essentially male and essentially female attributes are complementary to one another and should be celebrated not railed against. Rather than constantly digging around for evidence of unfairness, I think our efforts would be better aimed at looking for solutions not problems.

There are, of course, no physical signs that I have no children of my own so I can't avoid the question. I've even got the childbearing hips, which is a cruel thing to bestow on an infertile woman. I don't want to spit the words infertile, sterile, barren, infecund at anyone who chances to ask me a perfectly innocent question, but there are times when I want to say how it feels not to have you in my life.

I want it out in the open, but it's not an easy thing to just toss into conversation, not for me anyway. While I was living in the dreamland of a Dom reconciliation I did meet a woman who just came out with the fact that she was having fertility treatment. Inwardly, I applauded her frankness and you might have expected me to pitch in with my own experience, but I didn't. I held back. All I could manage was a sympathetic smile and the moment was lost. I feel ashamed even now of my inability to show support to a fellow sufferer. I could use the rawness of my separation as an excuse but it isn't good enough. Since that time I have tried to emulate her and casually drop the subject into conversation.

I remember an occasion when the topic was holiday jabs and the fear of needles became the theme. I chimed in about how I wasn't bothered by injections because I'd had so much experience of them during my fertility treatment days. I had an all-female audience and still the remark was met with an uneasy silence. Uncertain looks appeared on the faces around me, they didn't know what to do with the information. What were they supposed to say? What did I *want* them to say? To ask for more details about the treatment? An enthusiastic 'Oh do share what it's like to have fertility treatment Tess.' I don't think so. To murmur sympathy? Possibly, but it wasn't sympathy I wanted. Acknowledgement of having been through a difficult time? Perhaps, but to mention my infertility casually (like it didn't bother me) and *still* have it met with cool, shifty awkwardness was hurtful and has simply served to send me further underground.

We have unspoken guidelines on questions we don't ask of even our closest friends and family. Usually they relate to sex and money. I don't put the 'have you got children' question to any-one because I don't want to risk putting them through the same embarrassment or indeed distress that the question causes me. It is a conspiracy of silence.

It is after all our basic instinct to reproduce; too many like me and the future of our species looks bleak. Even the Bible doesn't go much on the barren; there are several accounts of infertile women and where they are sufficiently desperate, a miracle conception takes place. Forgive me a little 'Dot Cotton' moment here, Luke, Chapter one, verse 25. Elizabeth, an old woman (how old we're not told) finds herself to be 'with child'. 'Now at last the Lord has helped me,' she says. 'He has taken away my public disgrace.' In ancient Israel it was considered a sign of God's blessing to have children; to be childless therefore was not just sad, but as Elizabeth says, a 'disgrace'. Well, I don't feel as if I haven't been blessed, because in so many ways I have, and I certainly don't feel that I am a disgrace. However, infertility is life changing. It is stressful, painful and deeply upsetting and to have it ignored or brushed aside, diminishes the experience. Enduring the most arduous of treatments to join the parent club and to fail is tough and to be left on the periphery with apparently nothing to contribute towards the care of children is worse. I have at times wanted to wear my infertility as a badge of suffering for all I have been through, but I know that dragging my infertility around with me like a wooden cross, the smell of burning martyr filling the air, is not helpful. I feel it would be softer, nicer to share how I have imagined you in my life, though I'm not sure how that would be received; with a puzzled look probably.

So I find myself in a minority, a very often misunderstood minority, and it can be awkward but I don't feel the need to trumpet 'I'm barren but bodacious' or 'Sterile but sassy.' I don't want an outpouring of compassion either, just a simple nod of understanding.

'I do not want the peace which passeth understanding. I want the understanding that bringeth peace.' Helen Keller

While I struggle at times with my standing in society, as a woman without children, the simple fact I don't have you means I have a huge amount of room in my life for other people's children.

'There is no such thing as other people's children.' Hilary Rodham Clinton

Well Hilary, yes there is, but I think we know what she's getting at here. We are *all* responsible for the children in the world.

Parents can be forgiven for thinking that the childless aren't interested in their kids and children in general. Some childless people won't be, but I am. I love to hear about my friends' and relatives' children. OK, so occasionally in the past I might have stifled a yawn when a new mummy friend extolled the virtues of her broccoli munching offspring. Of course, I'm delighted the little nipper is getting a good dose of iron in his diet (or whatever it is that broccoli is exulted for) even though it might not be all *that* interesting.

During my years of 'trying' I often found it difficult to be around children and babies. The birth of a friend's child or of a niece or nephew was a bittersweet time for me, but now the hurt has faded I can share the joy of a new arrival and simply enjoy the company of children. Particularly joyful are the times when a child shows affection towards me or demonstrates a trust in me. The smallest of gestures can be a priceless treasure. I recently celebrated a birthday and wore a 'Super Auntie' badge all evening with the most ridiculous pride.

So how is it forming relationships with other people's children? The children who would have been your cousins and your friends. Well, it's not always straightforward. Des and I are careful. For a start it's not appropriate for us to force our affections on to the children in our lives, nor do we wish to buy their love by bestowing lavish gifts on them (though we often do). We simply strive to be significant adults in the lives of the children and young people that are dear to us. The role of confidant maybe or more gloriously as mentor. Certainly to be their champion and to support them feels good but we'd happily settle for just being thought of as a good laugh.

Naturally our relationship with the kids in our lives depends on our relationship with the children's parents. This connection can feel fragile at times; as any bond we have made with a child could easily be damaged or curtailed should our relationship with the parents break down. However, kids and young people seem to know when they are loved, perhaps an instinct for their own survival. We know our love for them is not the same as a parent's love and, of course, we know other people's children will never love us in the same way they love their mum and dad; and that's just fine. Love isn't a competition, one sort of love isn't preferable to another; it's enough to give it and receive it; no need to measure it.

We seek a simple relationship without duties or issues. It can be easier for kids and young adults to use another adult as a sounding board for a subject that might feel too daunting to broach with a parent; like the character Will, in Nick Hornby's[9] novel *About a Boy* (played by Hugh Grant in the film). Will has no responsibilities (not even a job) and befriends a boy and becomes his confidant. He understands the child's bullying problems at school while the boy's mother remains ignorant of her son's distress. Will doesn't offer any real solutions but simply being someone the boy can talk to is enough.

We love to hear of a person speaking of how they have felt about a special uncle or aunty or family friend. Ellen MacArthur's aunt helped her buy her first boat, a pretty significant gesture in that particular woman's life. Jools Holland got his love of Boogie-Woogie piano from his uncle Dave, again an important, inspiring influence. I wish I'd had an uncle to teach me Boogie Woogie piano rather than the stuff I was taught, 'Greensleeves' and the like. I have no idea what piano lessons are like these days; I would hope they would allow for some learning to play by ear and improvisation. For sure, if any of you kids had shown an interest I'd have bought a piano and done my best to find you a teacher who would enable you to play the sort of music you wanted to hear.

There aren't many very young children in our lives these days, but formerly with all the tidiness and ordered calm of just two

---

[9] This, I realise, is my second mention of Nick Hornby. I'm not surprised; I'm a huge fan and have read everything by him. His memoir *Fever Pitch* is quite the best way to understand a football fan.

adult residents, our home was nevertheless always prepared and ready for the onset of a band of children. I still have a large trunk containing children's games and colouring books which was once the 'go to destination' upon arrival of all our regular little visitors. The very existence of the trunk was a throwback from my own childhood, when my brothers and I kept all our toys in a large carved wooden coffer, which we called the 'The Treasure Chest' – how endearing. For certain I'd have had one for you.

In the past I have been guilty of going a bit over the top in my preparations for children's visits. I have tried (too hard probably) to get everything right, a need to demonstrate my ability to 'mother', to prove myself capable of looking after the children in my care. I've clipped articles from magazines on how to amuse kids on holidays and made sure I was equipped for wet or sunny days. I realise that this is because of my own insecurities and most probably my being oversensitive, for I have maternal instincts – why wouldn't I? I have always made sure that the children in my care are not stuffed full of sweets, crisps, Coke or burgers (I feel that's grandparent territory) but I'm not sure I'm really putting the needs of the child first here; to be truthful it's just me trying to absolve myself of criticism and if I'm honest to somehow prove my ability to 'mother'. However, as a result no parent has ever needed to fear for their children's health when they visit our home; there's no danger that a child will return home so high on caffeine and sugar that they won't settle. Besides Des would have usually wound them up sufficiently to make sure of that, so I've had no need to toss chemical additives into the equation.

Whenever a child writes me a note, sends me a card, draws me a picture or makes something for me, it means a great deal. Of course, parents are inundated with their offspring's scribblings. Kitchen walls and fridge doors are awash with tatty pieces of paper covered in blobs of garish felt pen and paint; inevitably a lot will find their way to the bin, but I keep them all, every one. All the thank-you letters, cards and postcards, the drawings and paintings. Some are quite faded and dog-eared, others I've had framed. I love the language of their world. I love the way smaller children can misjudge how much room they have for a sentence and have to squash the words together as the edge of the page looms, or, without a hyphen as apology, continue the word beneath. These items mean a lot to me, clearly more than the children will ever realise, and I thank those parents who have encouraged their children to produce these little treasures for me.

'I've never outgrown that feeling of mild pride, of acceptance, when children take your hand.' Ian McEwan, Enduring Love

Buying gifts for other people's children has always been and still is a great pleasure of mine, though I have to rein myself in at times. It wasn't always this way though. Children's departments used to feel like some sort of 'promised land'. Like an Aladdin's cave but without the magic lamp. I used to dream that one day, I too would be buying Spiderman pyjamas for you, my baby boy, and pink Tinkerbell sandals for you Lily. What a sexist mummy I would have been. I wanted to buy you books and especially those I had loved as a child. All the kids in my life get A A Milne's *Now We Are Six* when they reach that particular milestone; I wanted to buy it for you. I would also probably have driven you mad by foisting manuals and texts on you for any and every hobby or subject you'd shown an interest in.

It doesn't happen so much now, but in the past when I've been alone and gift shopping for kids I am ashamed to admit that if a shop assistant made the assumption that my purchases were for my own kids I didn't always correct them, for a brief moment I let myself inhabit my imaginary world of being a parent. Does that sound sad? It was a pointless behaviour and though harmless it always left me with an empty feeling afterwards; it was as if I was telling myself that being a non-mother wasn't enough.

In the past I have at times felt uneasy in the company of children, aware that I am trying too hard to do everything right, wanting to win their approval above all else. I have often found myself agonising over how I have been with the child. Should I have done more of this or less of that? How different I would have felt just being with you.

I'm not like this now. I have a more complete life as a non-parent and I am totally at ease with the young people in my life. I like to talk to children as equals for in my opinion children's wisdom by far exceeds our own. Children have so much to teach us about how to enjoy life to the full and making the most of every small thing. I think we pack away our childish ways far too early. I wonder what I might have learned from you.

At times I have tried to kid myself that my relationships with other people's children have been a salve for my childlessness; that they have helped me get over the fact that you never happened for me; but it just isn't so. The children and young people in my life are *not* the daughters and sons I never had; they could never, ever, be a substitute for you.

Being solely an imaginary parent does have its benefits. I have never had to say 'No' to you either screeched at the top of my voice or in a firm 'don't mess with me' tone that I'm sure I would have developed. I have never had to refuse requests for overpriced designer sunglasses or trainers. I've never denied you Cocopops or Coca-Cola. I've never made you eat Brussels sprouts or smoked haddock. I haven't dragged you screaming away from your Xbox/iPad/Facebook. I haven't spoiled you and turned you into money-grabbing greedy monsters because I've given in to you too often. Neither have I ever had to say to you that your daddy has moved out for some 'space'.

'Old age is an excellent time for outrage. My goal is to say or do at least one outrageous thing every week.' Maggie Kuhn

'The older one grows, the more one likes indecency.' Virginia Woolf

Yep, I'm with these two wise old birds and no children to embarrass. I am presently embracing a vision for myself as a slightly batty, irreverent, bawdy aunty. A 'giddy aunt' (love that phrase) maybe; I think it's a role that will suit me.

At the time of writing I am aunty to three teenagers and I happen to think teenagers are the best fun; I love their company, the language they use. Of course, I realise that the teenage years can be the most challenging for parents; I don't think I was an easy teenager to rear. I have called my childhood blissful and I think it was, but as I read through my teenage diaries there was a lot of angst going on, mostly about my appearance and relationships. Jeez what a boy obsessive I was.

I'm not sure how I would have coped with the challenge of setting boundaries in your teenage years. I haven't had to live with the fears that go with this maturing phase. The agonising waits for you to return home, much, much later than agreed; discovering drugs in your pockets when sorting out your laundry; learning that there will be older boys attending your girlie sleepover, Lily, and so on. I've avoided those exhausting rounds of negotiation and retribution, though I can't say I'm glad, obviously.

How would I have broached the subject of sex with you? I'd have bought a book, obviously, and I may have related to you the charming notion that when I was a young girl, my understanding of sex had been that it was only possible with love. As a result I hadn't been able to fathom how rape came about. I remember discussing this with a friend and we drew the conclusion that the rapist must feel love temporarily in order for the sex to take place but not afterwards. I don't recall when I realised this idea to be folly but I doubt children of your generation would have fallen for that illusion; that innocent perception would have been pretty much impossible in view of the extreme pornographic images that you might have been exposed to. I hope I would have ensured that you knew what was 'normal'…ish.

I remember an occasion as a teenager at school when a note was passed to a friend sitting next to me from the boys behind. It read, 'How do girls masterbate [*sic*].' At the time I hadn't discovered the practice but luckily my friend was more mature and sexually active and scribbled 'with your finger' and passed the note back. I laughed along knowingly. I was getting the idea but was glad to get home to a dictionary; it took a while to find the word because of the misspelling but enlightened I became with no loss of credibility. In the same vein when it fell to me a few years ago to explain to a nephew of mine what the 'Mile High Club' is all about, I was just glad that I might have saved him the humiliation of getting it wrong in the school playground.

I regret the things I cannot pass on to you my imagined children. The little details. The family things. The things I've learned through my own blissful childhood. I won't be passing on my version of my mother's technique for producing delicious, flavoursome, lump-free gravy[10] and to say, while I'm making it, as she often does, 'Gravy for the King's navy' (navy pronounced with an 'h' before the second syllable 'na-havy') for some reason I've never understood. I have asked my mother about this but she's unsure where it comes from. It sounds like a line from a Noël Coward play, but I've googled it and apparently not. Another of my mum's little tips is her method for stopping insect bites from itching – 'hot cross bun' them – that is, press your thumb nail firmly across the red swollen itchy bump one way and then another forming a cross – try it; it works, though it does actually hurt a bit so it's possibly just pain distracting from the itch. 'Suffolk' potatoes are another – a baked potato but without its jacket – crispy and delicious with butter and seasoned with salt and pepper.

Des and I have had to create rituals and traditions for our own family life of just we two, and it's fine. I wonder what rituals you would have brought to our lives; what would our family traditions have been? Christmas is a great time for family customs

---

[10] Mix around four parts plain flour to one part Bisto – yes Bisto, don't be sniffy about it, even Delia says it's only to add colour. For the two of us I use around one generously heaped tablespoon of the flour/Bisto combo, to which I add a little cold water and mix it to a smooth very thick liquid/paste. I then add a little water drained from vegetables and pour into the roasting tin the meat was cooked in (which should be coated in a yummy meat roasting residue), put on to heat, add a generous knob of butter and using a small whisk keep whisking the gravy and adding veg water until it is the thickness and quantity you desire. Don't be tempted to add wine or redcurrant jelly or some other on trend ingredient; it doesn't (in my opinion) enhance the flavour – just saying.

and Des and I have our own. First there is the tree selection; Des will patiently stand holding the stem of a Nordic spruce at our local garden centre for me to look at and we will then 'discuss' the shape, whether the space between the branches is sufficient and various other essential Christmas tree attributes, and after I have made sure we've sorted through and examined the entire stock we will eventually make a selection, which will invariably be the first one that Des picked out. We then decorate the tree to the sounds of Phil Spector's *A Christmas Gift to You.*

I am a traditionalist with regard to Christmas decorations, adhering to a strictly red, gold and green theme; no silver, purple or pink in our household and I'm not sure I would have conceded on this rule to accommodate your tastes, though something handmade by you would, whatever the hue, have been given a place to shine. I also love to bring the outside in and so copious amounts of greenery will be schlepped into the house from the garden and surrounding woodland. For a rather longer time than Des can tolerate, the house will be an uproar of squashed berries on the floor and random bits of twigs and leaves everywhere. Every year, as my homemade wreaths and garlands emerge triumphant I will make a vow not to leave it quite so late next year before I make them.

What would we have done with you in our lives? Would we have left carrots for the reindeers, mince pies and a glass of port for Father Christmas? Would I have made footprints of ash from the fireplace to your Christmas stockings with your father's wellie boots? Would I have kept my sense of humour when feeling exhausted by the pre-dawn awakenings of rowdy overexcited children? How would we have tackled the time when belief in the existence of 'Father Christmas' had waned? Of course, I don't know. Waking up on Christmas morning is often a quiet, reflective time for me and I often think of the contrast between our peaceful orderly home and those boisterous households full of children.

Christmas Eve is a day of food preparation in our household, which is the same for most I'm sure, and regardless of the numbers we are cooking for, even if it's just Christmas Dinner *à deux*, we will still do *all* the preparation the day before. This activity is usually accompanied by our *Carols from Canterbury Cathedral* CD and Des will do most of the veg prep while I make Delia's Traditional Eighteenth-Century Chestnut Stuffing (I've usually forgotten to get the ingredient mace and so I leave it out and it tastes just fine).

The Christmas roast dinner can be a stressful event in many households but it rarely is in ours because Des and I are so practised in the art of producing a roasty din. We *always* have a Sunday roast come rain or shine. On a blazing July day I can be found at my Aga mashing turnip (the Cornish word for swede) and stirring gravy (for the King's na-havy) and mostly I will be thinking that I am a lunatic and asking myself why we are not, like the rest of the population, lazily munching on a barbecued sausage outside in the sunshine. However, it has become such a part of our lives together that I think I would miss the ritual. Des is prep chef for the day so I really only pitch up at the gravy stage, so it's pretty much a day off for me. Des has become something of a figure of fun for his strict adherence to the Sunday roast but I have to admit I find a strange comfort in the routine of it; it feels grounding and reassuring somehow.

Talking of preparing vegetables brings to mind another tradition, which I have inherited from my mother, and she from hers, and it is called 'the stump'. This is the by-product of cauliflower preparation: the florets are cut away from the stalk in the usual way and we always add a few of the tender young leaves to the pot. The stalk is then trimmed of the tough edgy bits leaving the sweet raw inner, 'the stump', which for me is heaven to munch on. Des isn't partial to it so in our household I bag the whole of it. If my mother is staying with us, we share it. Maybe we would have shared it too and in your adult lives you might well have found yourselves asking when on cauli prep duty, if anyone wanted a piece of 'stump'; that would have made me smile.

What would we have done on Mother's Day? Would you have selected something for me from the pink wall of flowers and hearts that appear in all the supermarkets in early March. Would we have enjoyed an overpriced roast meal in an overcrowded local restaurant? Or would you have been a little more creative and if you weren't, would I have minded? I fear it has all gone a bit mad. I recall receiving an email from Apple one year about treating Mum to an iPad for Mother's Day – whaaat? Whatever happened to a bunch of daffs and a bar of fruit and nut, or breakfast in bed, or simply an offer to do the washing up?

Mother's Day has at times been an awkward day of sadness for me and mostly I have dealt with it by focusing on my own dear mum. I remember one occasion when Des and I took my late mother-in-law (and her elderly mother) out for lunch on Mothering Sunday and the very thoughtful restaurateurs gave each mother a little potted polyanthus to take home. I, of course, left empty handed and feeling excluded. I also felt mean. It was a nice gesture, very much appreciated by the mums present, so why did I have to turn it into a slight against me when it wasn't one? Gawd, I don't even like polyanthus.

'It takes a whole village to raise a child.' Bill Moyers

As a non-mother, can I pass any tips on to you, Lily, should you become a mother? Of course, I cannot tell you how it feels to be a mother but I can tell you how to relate to a childless friend and would also like to urge you not to become a whinging mom or a baby braggart.

All mothers are entitled to moan about the rigours of parenthood. It is relentless, energy-sapping hard work. It is all consuming, frustrating, expensive and at times overwhelmingly stressful. For some it can also be isolating. I am free of all this and must therefore live a charmed life. Yes I do. But hearing the moaning and whinging doesn't make me sigh with relief that I haven't got kids. It doesn't make me think of my infertility as a get-out-of-jail-free card.

Before I had fully accepted my childlessness I found the whinging particularly difficult to take from friends or family who knew of my situation. I once visited a friend who had just brought home her first-born. The child was asleep so I crept upstairs to the nursery to pay my first visit to this little baby girl. I stood silently by her cot and just looked at her, awestruck. Her perfect little features, the sound of her contented breathing, the smell of her skin. I just wanted to drink her in. It was also the first time I didn't feel the huge wrench of pain that seeing a small baby had brought me in the past. The longing was still there but at last I felt I was moving (albeit very slowly) towards acceptance of my lot and seeing this particular baby girl just made me feel wonder at the miracle of her very existence – apologies for the mushiness here but it was as if the contentment in that child had seeped into me. So, feeling all smiley and happy I returned to the company of the child's mother, who promptly destroyed my mellow mood by ranting about how 'trapped' she now felt by the perfectly formed, peacefully sleeping bundle upstairs. Trapped! I wanted to scream at her 'Look what you've got you ungrateful cow!' She was, of course, exhausted, hormonal and most likely struggling to cope with this needy living thing that she and her husband were now totally responsible for and quite possibly it was the first time the child had actually been sleeping peacefully since their return home. The remark voiced to another weary, first-time mum would have been quite acceptable; it just wasn't easy for me to hear. It might have been a 'heads-up', look Tess it really ain't that great. Perhaps all those who have moaned to me were simply trying to highlight the negatives of child rearing to make me feel better. It didn't work then and it still doesn't.

In fact, whining in general is a bore, isn't it? Negative people; a pain in the arse. It's the 'drains and radiators' thang with friendships. A little bit of advice here, children; those friends that suck the very lifeblood out of you bemoaning their lot, are to be avoided. This might sound harsh and it is much easier to say than to put into action but if you can, stick with the 'radiators', those who will encourage, support and energise you. These are the friends you will gladly support in the dark times as you will have sufficient energy to do so.

Quite naturally I find it easier to be in the company of parents who have clearly embraced the role. Parents who enjoy their children make me feel good, always have; even in the dark, longing, 'trying years'. It is no coincidence that my dearest, closest friends are such parents. It somehow justifies the pain I have felt from not being able to have my own. The whinging moms' lack of gratitude simply makes me feel I should have had the children *instead* of them. It's not appropriate to moan about aching legs after a long walk to someone in a wheelchair or to complain about the burden of an aging parent to an orphan. It's the old 'walk a mile in someone's moccasins' theme that keeps recurring in this letter. It's a lesson we should all learn and one I would have passed on to you; that it's a good idea to think about your audience before you open your mouth.

Parents who rejoice in their children are one thing, what I call the baby braggarts are quite another. I am sure many parents feel the same. Pride in being a parent is, of course, perfectly natural and a pleasure to witness but with some it can become a boast and that's when it becomes annoying. This 'bragging' can begin at conception, especially when it has happened with ease, or when the baby actually arrives, announced by a 'Baby on Board' sticker in the back of the car. It is mean of me, because, of course, it is a way of broadcasting to the world a joyful thing, becoming a parent, but when I was feeling raw and cheated it just felt like showing off. They are less prevalent these days and most are, or were, displayed with the best of motives. The parent simply has become very aware of what precious cargo they are carrying and, quite naturally, want to do as much as possible to ensure safe passage for their child. Though the premise that the notice is there to ensure people allow a greater braking distance because there is a little person on the back seat is, I suspect, not always its purpose (as I write those words I just *know* that it is not about health and safety). Would a sign saying 'Frail old Granny in the back' require the same level of care I wonder? Should I sport a 'Bash my bumper I'm barren' sticker? Am I sounding bitter? Yes I know I am, because it is, of course, all to do with celebrating fertility – what could possibly be wrong with that? Hell, that did sound bitter! Would I have been tempted to sport a 'Baby on Board' sticker had you arrived? Naa– too naff. Would I have coveted a state-of-the-art pushchair? Yes!

A particularly tedious hobby of the baby braggart is to boast of their child's achievements. Of course, for the majority of parents their child is *the* most attractive, *the* most intelligent, *the* funniest, *the* quickest (or all of these things), but it is one thing to boost a child's confidence, quite another to create a child with a head so large that it won't fit through a door.

There are many aspects to parenting today that I really don't envy and one in particular is what I call 'competitive parenting'. The 'boasters' have always been around, but 'competitive parenting' seems a relatively new phenomenon. There are numerous television programmes telling parents how to 'parent'. What their children should be eating; what time to put them to bed; how to discipline them and so on. I'm not sure what my response to the childcare gurus would have been. I'm pretty sure I would have read some books on the subject but it saddens me that parents are not presumed to have an instinct for the job any more, when, of course, they do. The application of common sense, which seems to have departed from almost every aspect of our daily lives, is only deemed appropriate if it's been written down in a manual or directed by a childcare expert on BBC3. The result is that when a toddler decides to let rip in a supermarket aisle the poor mother who does nothing is often reviled instead of pitied. Likewise if a desperate mother administers a mild tap to the back of a child's legs, she is likely to be set upon by a crowd of well-meaning adults. As a non-parent I don't ever feel entitled to comment on such 'bad parenting' antics – if that's what they are. It's a difficult area with uncertain boundaries. Of course, any violence directed at a child should always be deemed as mistreatment but what about passing on an eating disorder to a child? Is that not also some form of abuse? Would it be OK to intervene when a yo-yo dieting mother deems her 'puppy fat' child as overweight? Or those 'kind' mothers who show their love by fattening their children with home-baked goodies and treats? I suspect not.

I know my own mother did follow her instincts. I remember an anecdote she told me of when my older brother was a tiny baby; she'd taken him to the child health clinic of the day and the nurse had wanted him to be undressed and weighed. My mother refused as it was a cold day and he was all wrapped up, cosy and happy. Would I have done the same with you? I don't know, but

I am sad to admit I think you might have been unwrapped and weighed with me, 'Mrs Compliant Mummy', biting her lip, or maybe a deep concern for your welfare would have emboldened me to speak up for you, if not for myself.

Do I judge the way my friends and family members parent? I try not to, but at times I'll disagree with what they are doing – natural enough surely but parenting like many other aspects of life is an individual thing not to be interfered with (unless, of course, we are talking about real abuse). So much more is expected of parents today. Parenting has become a much more complicated process; the development of children is constantly measured and analysed. The Bill Moyers quote that '*it takes a whole village to raise a child*' seems to apply to our society less and less. It seems that governments direct (dictate?) how children should be raised and then leave the parents solely responsible for every aspect of their child's upbringing. Teachers can only educate within the strict parameters of the curriculum. Their powers of discipline are diminished and their ability to provide comfort to a distressed child removed for fears of abuse. The police too have to tread very carefully around our junior population for fear of violating a child's rights. There was uproar a while back when three teenage girls were detained at a police station for several hours having been caught vandalising public property with graffiti. The parents protested over the violation of the girls' rights; this being the 'right' to vandalise without due punishment presumably. It seems the disciplining of children by anyone other than the parent can be problematic. It is a delicate area, yet a mild telling off of a child who is misbehaving is surely permissible, welcome even.

As a non-parent I feel I have no right to say my views out loud, what do I know? I cannot join the motherhood club, my lack of qualification stands in the way and cannot be waived. However, when *asked* for advice, I will make a contribution to discussions on child rearing but I will still be *very* careful with my words, measured and mindful, never critical and mostly I think it best just to be a listening ear. I can certainly remember being a child. I have a very good memory for things in my past so there must be something to glean from my childhood surely, but I know it's not my place to comment if I disapprove of the way a friend is parenting, though nor is it that of a parent.

'The hard truth is that if you aren't enjoying your parenting, your child isn't enjoying being a child.' Randy Colton Rolfe

It is OK to assume that good parenting skills don't always come naturally but loving the child surely does. But here lies the taboo for the fertile. Some parents clearly do not enjoy their membership of the parenthood club; some appear to wish they'd never joined at all. When it is more than just feeling trapped on occasion or frustrated with the drudgery and routine demands, it must be unsettling and confusing. I imagine those who find the whole parenthood thing is really not for them feel just as isolated as the infertile. It is extremely difficult to come 'out' and say it's not for you. The child exists for God's sake; there is no real option to cancel membership. It is OK to say that you can't cope, the rash of toddler training books and television programmes acknowledge that parenting can be a tough job, but to admit that you don't actually like your child is unacceptable. Very often this feeling can be attributed to post-natal depression, if it is not, then most likely anyone finding themselves in this situation will be driven underground. Lionel Shriver's novel *We Need to Talk about Kevin* was shocking in that it broke this taboo and has empowered some women to come out but nevertheless leaves them feeling that this lack of connection with their child is their fault. Luckily the scenario is rare and I would hope even more unusual in the parents of a child brought about via a long stint on the fertility treatment treadmill. I cannot imagine anything more disturbing or distressing than finding that post arduous infertility procedures, the mother/child bond isn't there. Less rare are those parents who love their children, don't regret having them, but nevertheless mourn the passing of their childfree lives; again this is not a subject openly discussed.

As I write this letter to you there are more and more organisations emerging that non-mothers can belong to. Thankfully there are now 'can't have kids' clubs and 'women without toddlers' groups available. Organisations that involuntarily childless women like me can join and offload about being childless. Like many minority groups the World Wide Web is the best place for like-minds to be found. The organisation Gateway Women can be a sanctuary for women like me and its emergence delights me, and there are chat rooms aplenty geared towards women still on the treatment trail and those just leaving it. There are also sites and bloggers for those of us who have reached the acceptance zone.

I haven't made any online connections with like-minded women. I'm not sure why, it might be because I have you, but it's good to hear the voices of other childless women, if only to know that I am not alone. I have held back from offloading my own stuff online but I recognise I have a need to unburden myself and that is being met by my writing to you.

'Making light of something heavy makes it easier to bear.'
Stephen Fry

I agree with the eloquent Mr Fry and I would like to share my experience with others on a lighter level. In the same way the motherhood club members will talk of their childbearing/rearing issues; so can the infertile. We could perhaps spend a wine-fuelled evening joshing about vaginal ultrasounds and egg collection, inhaling Buserelin, and hormone injections. I know from my time at the Breakthrough group for separated people that a shared experience is an instant bonder whatever that experience may be. However I know of no one in or around my social circle who has had the same experience as me; the conspiracy of silence again.

Quite naturally I struggle at girlie gatherings when an exchange of childbirth anecdotes takes place. I still want to crawl away and hide. Mercifully as middle age creeps in, this situation happens less and less, but the subject matter, that of stitches, sore nipples, leaking from various orifices and the various forms of pelvic floor damage, makes me feel (obviously) like a total outsider. I actually want to be invisible and mostly I am. I accept that when I'm among a group of mothers they wouldn't be concerned about the one without. The fact that I have been among friends at these times makes my isolation more keenly felt. I sometimes wonder if I chipped in a remark about stretch marks whether they would even notice. As I write this I know that they would; I can see the puzzled looks and hear the strained silent response now. I'd be like some sort of infiltrator. Perhaps this is why I prefer male company, the banter between them, the conversation topics will never cause me such discomfort.

So, it is difficult for the infertile and the fertile to truly empathise with one another's experience. Does this matter? Probably not. The only time it matters is when the sharing of the good news of a pregnancy is tainted. Just post my first IVF failure I met one of my closest friends for lunch. She told me she was expecting her second child and promptly burst into tears. Wailing that it should have been me. We both experienced such a mixture of emotions. Her compassion towards me made me feel all warm and loved but at the same time I felt angry that my situation had tainted what should have been a joyful announcement for my friend; a shared cause for celebration had instead become a time for tears. I'm glad to say not one of my friends or family has ever hidden a pregnancy from me. They might have dreaded telling me but tell me they always did. I have never had to suffer the shock, like many of those in the ranks of the 'still trying', of learning that a friend (who you'd just thought was putting on a bit of weight) was, in fact, six months pregnant.

A life without children affects one's status in the world. 'The mother of my grandchildren' carries more weight than 'my son's wife'. We live in a society where the child is king. A culture where the child and parent are worshipped. This is as vital as it is to be fertile (chest-beatingly proud of it or otherwise). It is essential for the continuation of our species, but hell, it doesn't half make those of us in barrenville feel a little superfluous. Hearing of an untimely death is always more tragic if that person is a parent, of course it is, there are children to consider, more people left grieving. Grief by volume. But there is no escaping the message here: the life of a childless person is worth less. That's hard to accept sometimes.

I was tempted to cross out the above paragraph, because of the 'pity me' connotations. Of course, the friends and family of the childless mourn them when they shift off their mortal coils. How you have lived your life, the people you have touched, simply loving others, affect the way you are remembered rather than how many offspring you've managed to bring into the world. I'm not sure, but I think the issue here might be that the childless leave nothing physical of themselves behind. Not one of you, my children, will walk the earth with my smile, my eyes, my messy hair or my mannerisms. None of you will find yourselves repeating phrases you've heard me say or pass on my technique for creating lump-free gravy. Is that important to me? To leave my mark on the planet? I think not; life always goes on.

Back to Bill Moyer's quote of it taking a whole village to raise a child, my knowledge of anthropology is extremely limited and based on having watched the odd documentary on tribal peoples across the world. I refer to the ones where it is the job of *all* the women of the community to care for the younger children while the men are off hunting and gathering with the older male children. I'm not saying it's a society hierarchy we should be returning to but the roles are clearly defined. Ours have become blurred. We're so pleased with our society that is so rich in its choices, and yet it can also mean that a mother can find herself struggling at home alone while at the same time a childless woman like me can find herself an untapped resource in an excluding community.

I want to make you aware too, that conversely the childless can also feel used, most especially in the workplace. I have a childless friend who is Head of a large secondary school, a demanding role and one she is passionately committed to. Throughout her career it has often been assumed that she has more time to give because she hasn't got children. She has stayed behind on late duties more than enough times, because her work colleagues have got to be home 'because of the kids'. The assumption being that my friend has nothing more important demanding her presence elsewhere – what could be more important than children? Of course, she has had things she would rather do, but it is hard to argue for time for herself against those who are asking for time for their children.

The childless are often scorned in this way. Lack of experience with children mocked. I've heard more than once, 'You can tell he/she hasn't got children.' It can sound like a smug affirmation of their superior role. The trouble is, it's true. I don't know what it's like to have children, but I wanted to know and to be made to feel inadequate around children always hurts. I often hear of how becoming a parent has changed a person's worldview and how they live their lives. Of course it does, like any major event in our lives; it shapes us. Probably words like 'responsible' and 'mature' would crop up here and, of course, 'love'. Finding within yourself this huge, mahoosive cloud of love for a precious offspring and being taken aback by the power of it. The enormity of it. The boundlessness of it. The specialness of it. The profoundness of it. I could go on. Am I trying to show you that I know what that love feels like? No I'm not. I can only imagine it.

I used to get angry when I heard sentences that began with 'Now that I am a parent, I do/feel/see X differently.' Comments like, once you have kids you become a universal parent; that parenthood brings a different set of emotional sensitivities; that being a mother means a greater empathy for other mothers. I have wanted to rail at these women and say that, of course, I ache too when I see a starving child in a drought-scarred African landscape; that the sight of a kid scavenging for food on some rubbish tip in South America will make my heart break too. I will be blubbing and calling Children in Need with my credit card number when I hear the story of an eleven year old in Glasgow who is carer for her bed-ridden mother. I will also weep when I see a photograph of beautiful baby boy washed up on a beach in Turkey. I fear I have been too sensitive in viewing such remarks as an implication that as a non-mother I would feel less; I'm sure that wasn't the intention. My anger in the past I think was from my frustration at feeling excluded. I tried to convince myself that by using my vivid imagination I could *know* how it feels to be a mother; but I now know that to be a falsehood. I am ready to admit defeat. I am no longer battling to have a status I cannot own; it's a gentle acceptance only now settling within me. I love you my imagined children, but I *cannot* know what it feels like to love my own, real, living child and it's a hollow sentiment to say out loud.

'Gay men are the only group of people who aren't looked down upon if they don't have kids.' Elton John

Elton, of course, now has children of his own. He is also, I imagine, godfather to many. I am godmother to four children. Each time it has felt an honour and a privilege. However, until I'd fully accepted my lot as 'non-mother', it always felt like something of a consolation prize in a raffle; the meal for two instead of the car. Naturally this was most keenly felt when I was actually undergoing treatment. I'd attend the baptism ceremony, all the time wishing I were the mother, even if the child was bawling his or her head off.

The definition of godparent in the *Oxford English Dictionary* is this: 'A person, who in various Christian Churches, traditionally takes responsibility for the Christian upbringing or education of a person being baptized, and (if the latter is a child) makes the promises on behalf of the child at the baptism ceremony.'

I've checked out these promises on the little cards I have for my godchildren. It seems praying for them regularly is a requirement and 'giving them encouragement to follow Christ and to fight against evil' (the latter sounds a bit daunting).

Whatever the religious sensibilities, being a godparent should give you a unique connection with the child. I think this is especially so if they are not family members as it is a demonstration of what that friendship means, a clear indication that you are valued in their lives.

In my opinion a childless person is a particularly good choice for a godparent. They are more likely to take the responsibility more seriously and they have most likely got more energy to direct at the child since they are not exhausted and haggard from the excesses of raising their own. I guess potentially too, they may have more money, though obviously not the infertile still on the treatment trail (and paying for it themselves).

The role seems less meaningful today. It was previously a job for life but I have to confess to having lost touch with one of my godchildren. On a cynical note, a lot of baptisms do seem to be a good excuse for a party when, due to the arrival of the child, nights out with friends have been few and far between. Baptisms in some cases are purely as a means to get a child educated in a particular school (ahem). All the more need for a godparent with such sinners for parents.

'Many children, many cares; no children, no felicity.'
Christian Nestell Bovee

So, as I have missed having you in my life so much, why haven't I adopted a child or two? Adoption is often thought of as the next step post unsuccessful fertility treatment. It's the ultimate cure for infertility. An instant child without all those drugs and trips to the hospital. So why haven't I got a tribe of adopted children running through my home?

Dom and I did have a meeting at an adoption agency and it was made clear to me then that I would need to be at the stage where I had let go of the idea of my own biological child, let go of you, before any moves towards adoption could take place. The meeting was between IVF attempts so I was still very much hoping to bring you into my life. The main reason for attending the meeting was to find out about the procedure and what it entailed. Dom's sister, Laura, was adopted and a better advert for a happy adoption outcome you would be pressed to find. So quite naturally we were very positive about adoption as a possibility for us.

We were told that it was unlikely that we would be able to adopt a child under the age of five, which was a disappointment but not unexpected. We were also aware that it could be a lengthy process and thought it might be prudent to get our names on a waiting list, should the quest for our own child fail. I also admit that part of me hoped that we might adopt and then go on to have our own biological child with ease, the sort of scenario you hear of, most likely via the tabloids, as happening a lot; whether it does or not I don't know. At the time I didn't really understand the requirement to have fully let go of the need for you before embarking on the adoption procedure. I do now.

The need to have moved well and truly on from fertility treatment is clear to me. The desire to conceive a child has to be separated from the desire to raise a child to enable successful adoption. If I were still hankering after my own biological child, an adopted child would always seem like second best. Hardly a healthy way to start a relationship with a child, especially with one that is likely to have security issues.

Adopting a child out of a sense of obligation or guilt is never going to be the best premise either. When I sit in front of a TV documentary on adoption with its images of delightful little kids desperate for a family I am torn and heartbroken. I look at the children, who have invariably been shifted from one place to another in their short little lives, and imagine bringing one of them home. Watching these children learning to accept that the family they were born into, for some reason or another can no longer be their family, is unbearably sad, made worse by the fact that I know we could show them what a loving family life could be like; and then the doubts crowd in. Could Des and I provide a loving home and stable environment in which to nurture these children and help them overcome their poor start in life? Yes I'm sure we could. So why don't we? Why haven't I replaced you with real children?

There was quite a gap between my last lot of fertility treatment and then meeting and committing to my new partner. Marrying at the onset of our middle age it felt like Des and I were somehow too set in our ways for adoption to work. It simply felt too late. For me the key to accepting my infertility has been to embrace the advantages of being childfree. It is difficult to turn that on its head and adopt a child. We've created a life without children that we love and we are reluctant to threaten that. Images of needy children desperate for a loving family make me feel guilty and selfish for continuing to live my life untouched by the disruption a child can bring, but do the parents of just one child ever feel the pressure to adopt? I somehow doubt it. They can, of course, alleviate the guilt by considering the possible disruption to the life of their existing child. A valid reason perhaps and a much more comfortable one than being worried about the disruption to your own life

The procedures towards adoption are necessarily invasive too. Home visits, vetting and assessments of your lifestyle and commitment to parenting. It has to be this way; maniacs and abusers can never be allowed to slip through the net, but the hoops that have to be got through are daunting. To accept the necessary prying into personal circumstances requires a big commitment to adoption at the outset, which is probably why it is so. The actual adoption will demand even more commitment.

I did once meet a woman at a party who had just adopted two little girls (they were siblings). She was thrilled and excited as she talked of them. It left me feeling ashamed, a coward, a fraud. Why hadn't I adopted? It felt like I'd failed at that too.

Clearly adoption raises many uncomfortable questions for me and the most important one I think, is why did I want to have children in the first place? Was it a need to nurture? A way of giving purpose and meaning to my life? For me these needs can be satisfied in other ways. In my opinion the answer to deciding whether or not to adopt should be a clear establishment that these needs *cannot* be met in any other way.

I have heard it said of the involuntarily childless who decide against adoption that this is clearly an indication that their need for children could not have been strong enough in the first place. An insult quite frankly. It doesn't mean you don't want children or need them. It might be selfish but I'll say it out loud – I just wanted my own child. My own baby made of him and me. I wanted you. I hoped that you might inherit the best of me and the best of my man. It didn't seem like too much to ask.

So, how did I come to accept that I would never actually meet you? Never be your mum and yet still be happy.

'Once we accept our limits, we go beyond them.' Brendan Francis

Well, it seems to me that we are expected to get over things quickly these days, move onwards and upwards as fast as possible. Sometimes I think we need a good deal more time to fully understand what happens to us and how it makes us feel. I needed to understand why I wanted a child so badly, beyond that of natural maternal instinct. I also needed to understand how it felt to have that craving denied. To land in this positive place beyond childlessness has required a shift in focus. To move away from a life pining for a baby has been a very gradual process; it's not just like stepping over a line. It's been a slow acceptance of a role that embraces the advantages of not having children, while still acknowledging the odd shot of pain of never having known you.

I've never done this as an aid to recovery but I could make a list of the disadvantages that having children can bring. The fact that children can be horrible. They can be rude, ungrateful, dismissive, manipulative, unkind, scheming, insulting, thoughtless and selfish. Expensive to run is another drawback. I've just googled it and apparently it costs £222,458 to raise a child.

Not only must the costs be borne but the inconvenience too. A childless trip to the beach for me would involve taking a book, a tube of Piz Buin, a bottle of water and a towel. As your parent I would be required to lug boogie boards, buckets and spades, drinks, food, extra clothes for weather changes or accidents, grown-up sun oil and a large bottle of kiddie sun block too. I might stuff a magazine in one of the numerous bags but it wouldn't get read because of all the time spent keeping an eye on you, checking that you weren't getting out of your depth in the water, talking to strangers or generally straying. However,

I would have been able to watch you achieve the milestone of swimming unaided for the first time. I could also have shared your joy at the first little fish caught in a net and snapped a pic of your first enthusiastic sandcastle construction. I'd have liked that.

There are advantages too for the home of the childless. More money to spend on it in the first place and colour schemes I like; you know I hate all those bright primary-coloured plastic accessories that are *never* put away, and we're spared the later hell-hole of the teenage bedroom (walls painted a nice gothic black). The childless car has no extra unsightly kiddie chairs, neither is it the skip on wheels that so many young family vehicles inevitably become, with sweet wrappers, felt pens with missing lids, bits of toys and other sundry rubbish scattered everywhere you look. Having said that I know I would have made you gather your rubbish. I hope that I wouldn't have turned sour too many happy childhood moments with a nagfest about mess and your duty to tidy but it would have been an element of our lives together for sure.

Des and I can have any conversation about what we want whenever the mood takes us; we haven't had to wait until you are in bed to have adult conversations. We can be spontaneous. We can go out whenever we want. No babysitters required – though conversely that also means the non-availability of the 'Would love to come but we can't get a sitter' excuse.

While I said to you that I might have hankered to be a 'yummy mummy', I am grateful there was never any pressure on me to be one. Thank goodness, as it is a ridiculous expectation that, post childbirth, the new mother should emerge triumphant with a stomach as flat as a washboard (from intensive Pilates) and without a leaking nipple or a grubby muslin square (flopped over shoulder) in sight.

In my 'trying' days this list of disadvantages would have been wiped out at a stroke by simply hearing 'I love you Mummy.'

I have no experience of the difficulties having kids can present, the physical strains of carrying them in pregnancy and the sheer unutterable agony of bringing them into the world in the first place. I will never know the emotional ups and downs of raising you through all the phases of your lives. The terrible twos, the toddler tantrums, the teenage rebellions, adolescent angst and the grief that accompanies the ultimate flight from the nest. My marriage will not be subject to the potential strain that introducing children can effect. Would your arrival have made or broken my partnership? I will never know.

'Families with babies and families without babies are sorry for each other.' Edgar Watson Howe

I find I can't agree with this quote. I have never felt sorry for any of the families in my life with babies. I know friends have felt sorry for me living my life without you but I'm also sure that at times they've envied me my orderly, clutter free, childfree existence. I have quite naturally at times envied the families of others. I watch a child cuddle into his or her mother and I ache to feel that kind of love from you. I remember an experience as a child when we were visiting the home of some childless friends of my parents. They were an honorary aunty and uncle, since we didn't use first names for adults when I was a child. I was fond of them. They kept colouring books and crayons especially for our visits in a drawer in an old sideboard, in the same way I do now. I recall cuddling into a pair of legs I thought belonged to my mother. I heard a voice above me say, 'Oh that's nice dear.' It was not the voice of my mother, horrified at my mistake I let go as if I had been burned. I've said this before but I think it bears repetition: I know that I can never get close to being loved by a child in the same way its mother is. I don't expect it and it doesn't make me sad. It is just how things are.

I would have loved to talk to the woman I was aged between twenty-eight and thirty-three, my 'trying' self. I'd like to say to her, 'You can have a joyful life without that baby' but I know I wouldn't have listened. I was only interested in stories of miracle babies, babies against all odds stories, not the tales of those who ended up without. But with hindsight I am sure I would have used the tools I now have to look for a richer life beyond the baby obsession.

'Parents are often so busy with the physical rearing of children that they miss the glory of parenthood, just as the grandeur of the trees is lost when raking leaves.' Marcelene Cox

So what sort of mother would I have been? I'm sure I would have been a very affectionate huggy, kissy sort, which would, particularly for you my boy(s), have been excruciating in your teenage years. Hopefully I would have learned to back off until the time when you found it acceptable to hug your mother and maybe if I was lucky enough tell me that you loved me. Whether you liked it or not I would never have held back from telling you that I loved you; *all* of the time. It sounds simple and real parents might disagree but I believe as long as any child knows that he or she is loved *unconditionally* they will be just fine. So while I know there would have been times when that love would be tested, the challenge of parenthood is, I believe, to make sure the love is always there.

I often wondered how motherhood would have changed who I am. Of course, I will never know, but I think in relation to the daughter that I am and the friend that I am, it means I would simply have had less time for those roles. So I'll tell you about me, who I am and as I write I might discover the parts of me that motherhood might have changed and how aspects of my personality might have manifested in your lives. I'll share some of the lessons I have learned, and those I'm still learning. I'll talk some more about my values, my loves and my hates. However, I don't want this letter to end up reading like a social media profile with lists of favourite films,[11] books, music and so on as any of my 'favourites' lists can alter with my mood, the season or the current fashion or trend.

So what other loves of my life would tell you more about me and who I am? I love anything essentially British, our traditions and idiosyncrasies. I'll give you an example: the State Opening of Parliament, when Black Rod knocks on the door of the Commons and has it slammed in his face to symbolise the Commons' independence. I love it. I also love the fact that this hilariously eccentric ceremony is always televised. The way it is carried out with such gravitas; we all know the door is going to be slammed shut but still dear old Black Rod keeps knocking until eventually the door is opened. I love the pomp and ceremony of our state occasions; it is I think a thing that we Brits do so very well. I *love* this country that I live in with a passion and I wouldn't want to live anywhere else. I hope you would have loved your lives here too, though I suspect you may have been frustrated at my latent timidity for travel. I blame Cornwall for

---

[11] I do feel the need to mention how I love the Bourne films – I watch them over and over which astonishes Des as I hate violence with a passion. It is, of course, the Matt Damon factor that explains this quirk.

this lack of wanderlust. Since I have lived here my appetite for trips abroad has all but disappeared.

I love words, so naturally enough for me I love my dictionaries; I own several. I've mentioned my slang dictionary before as a love of mine; my penchant for colourful, colloquial language. I have a couple of 'Writers' dictionaries and my beloved two big fat volumes *The New Shorter Oxford English Dictionary*. The paper in these heavy books is oh so thin, not quite tissue, almost biblical, i.e. like the quality of paper in a bible. They're so delicate and I love flicking through for word definitions. It's so much more satisfying than any app you could name, as you can come across interesting words you weren't looking for and can waste hours.

So, I love words; I love reading them and I love writing them down. Words and writing have led me to a bit of a fetish for stationery. I love notebooks and am very particular about mine. They must have plain covers, of either black, grey or kraft paper. They must have smooth blank pages. Never present me with anything ruled, the lines feel constricting and besides my writing is too big to fit between them.

Pens, quite naturally, are another passion. I write with fountain pens mostly, sometimes rollerball pens and always those with a fine nib or point, and I'm talking extra fine – the sort they tell me is really only suitable for precise figure work and not intended for general writing. I always write in dark brown ink, I love the 'sepia' look. I will avoid biros at all costs, their sole use in my life is for signing the back of credit cards or when I've chosen a greeting card for someone which is made of annoying shiny paper which my pens won't write on (arrgh). This leads me to another stationery-linked passion of mine, that of greeting cards. I always have a huge stash of them for each and every occasion.

I especially like to have sympathy cards on standby, which may sound gloomy but I'm always keen to respond quickly when receiving sad news. I take particular care over the words I use on these occasions, even when the person that has died was very very old and perhaps their quality of life diminished, their passing will still leave a huge empty space for their loved ones and I always try to respect that fact. I always include something positive about the person, or share a happy memory that I hope will provide some small comfort.

I've mentioned baking as a fairly new-found passion but I haven't told you that while baking I am always accompanied by Radio 4. It's another love and I listen whenever I can. I especially enjoy the book programmes, the afternoon play (not always, sometimes they're not up my *straße*), *The Archers* and *Woman's Hour* (I particularly like presenter Jane Garvey, she sounds like someone I could go for a pint with). Sometimes Radio 4 can annoy me, it can get very 'up its own arse' at times and on occasion I cringe at its middle-classiness. I can also feel out of my depth with it; Melvyn Bragg's *In Our Time* is so intellectually above me that I feel like the butter spatula in the knife drawer whenever I tune in. *Gardeners' Question Time* I love though I miss John Cushnie (a forthright and funny presenter who sadly died in 2009).

This neatly brings me on to my love of gardening. In particular the smells involved. The smell of roses gives me joy; no point I believe, in growing a rose that isn't scented. Sweet peas smell heavenly and dear lavender. I love, love, love the smell of lavender and always have. I scoff at those who deem it an old lady smell; now that I am one it doesn't matter anyway.

The smell of the earth as I'm weeding makes the task a pleasure. For me the aroma of a freshly pulled leek or spring onion combined with mother earth is sublime. Another touch of the eccentric coming through possibly when I can be spotted sniffing a bunch of recently harvested shallots from my potager. I don't know why I've written the word potager, perhaps I should have written 'kitchen garden' but again that's not what I call it in reality. Actually I do know why, I'm trying to sound posh. A contradiction in the personality of someone who likes looking up rude words in a slang dictionary. It is my veg patch, though I feel that the label doesn't do justice to the wonder that is my beloved raised-bed, gravel-pathed vegetable garden where I labour to grow food and cut flowers.

I don't wear old scuddy clothes to garden in. In addition to my need for full make-up at all times (or at least a lick of mascara and under eye dark circles concealer), I also like to wear clothes I feel good in, even when I'm getting hot and sweaty wheeling barrows of compost around. I have a keen interest in fashion and love getting frocked up. Sadly my lifestyle does not lend itself to too many glitzy occasions so often I find myself feeling a tad overdone in my local pub, but I find with old age I care less and less and these days glam up regardless of whether I look like I've tried too hard or that I belong somewhere else – that somewhere else is clearly a more glittering place. I absolutely love clothes and do actually refer to my wardrobe as my child substitute. I'm not saying that my love for clothes is in any way as intense as the love I have for you, of course not; simply that the money that would have been spent on you, goes on clothes. How much did I say it costs to raise a child? £222,458; umm, not actually enough.

'I like my money right where I can see it – hanging in my closet.' Sex and the City

I wonder whether you would have shared that passion with me, Lily? Would we have enjoyed the shopping trips for clothes that I enjoy with my own mother? I like to think you might have liked my wardrobe and me yours. We might have lent each other things, though I have to confess here that I am not a happy lender. I will do it but I struggle with the idea. I look after my things and am never quite sure I can trust another person to do the same and am therefore uncomfortable until its safe return. I'm not a happy borrower either; I'd rather buy my own book/sander/paint sample/leather jacket/hat.

Would you have deemed any of my clothes wearable? I like to think you would, but as I said there would have been tension if you'd chosen to borrow anything precious until the garment returned home unscathed. Of course, we might not have been the same size, Lily, so it might never have come up. I'd like to have a little bleat on the subject of size here; since when did a size 12 become 'curvy'? And we all know that curvy is polite parley for fat. How did sizes get so small?[12] How can anyone really be a size zero? I was shopping recently with a friend in the iconic Oxford Street Top Shop store when my friend commented: 'Tess, I believe we have strayed into the children's department.' We also later mused that these establishments should perhaps design an entrance threshold with a slender doorway, so that if you couldn't actually prise your body through the gap to gain entry then it is probable that that particular store would hold no stock to fit you. Or maybe they could have an alternative wider doorway labelled with a warning 'This Entrance is for Purchasers of Accessories Only'. That way you could go straight to the shoe/handbag section and save yourself the humiliation of searching for clothes that might fit a 'curvy' size 12. Another note on sizes; it is just a number. I know women who won't buy a garment if the size that fits them is bigger than their normal size – lunacy.

---

[12] Girlie Fashion Tip: Buy knickers one or two sizes up – they will fit just fine and give a smoother line (no digging in).

The variation in sizes is enormous and it seems to me entirely random. Wear the size that fits you – cut the number 18 out of it if it makes you feel better and *never* wear anything that's too tight. Of course, Lily, we might not have shared the same taste either; quite possibly I would have inwardly squirmed at some of your outfit choices. I say 'inwardly', but I'm not sure if I would have remained silent. I don't think I could have resisted putting on my Gok Wan hat from time to time. I guess if you were a sporty girl, wearing lycra, or baggy T-shirts and tracky bottoms all the time, I would have shrugged and given up…eventually. I think I would have been easy to manipulate in a fitting room though; seeing you looking fab-u-lous in something wildly expensive would have been hard for me to resist.[13]

I'm not excluding you boy(s) here. I hope you would have been interested in fashion too or at least in your appearance, though I have to say I prefer men to have an effortless style, or at least one that 'appears' effortless. The 'try hard' is never a good look.

Can we talk about tattoos? Umm, if any of you had wanted one, I just know I would have googled for photos of the old and saggy looking ghastly and would have hoped that would be a deterrent. However, I have just done exactly that only to find some images of tattooed oldies looking pretty darn fine, so that would have backfired.

---

[13] General Fashion Tip: When purchasing a garment that has ribbons at the neck (in order to keep the item safely on the hanger while on display) please cut them off before wearing, they are not supposed to be visible. Whenever I see them poking out of someone's neckline I want to advance on them with a pair of scissors.

Beauty products are another drain on my finances. I will almost slavishly purchase any recommendations from beauty writers I admire like India Knight, Sali Hughes and Caroline Hirons. The more lavishly packaged these products are the better; of course, it's a ghastly waste of money and resources, but it just makes the whole purchasing process so much more of a pleasure.[14] When a beauty product really works or is simply a pleasure to use it improves my day no end. I look better with make-up and as I'm sure I have said before, to me, looking good is feeling good, so quite why some women are sniffy about make-up I don't know. I feel there is a profound sense of honour in looking after yourself and for me that includes a beauty routine.[15] I am now at the age where the focus is on anti-aging products. To be honest the wrinkles I have don't overly concern me, though I do slap on the hallowed Boots No7 Protect&Perfect serum most days and I would have recommended to you to use a sun protection factor on your face of around 50 all year round. I regularly scour the press to find new and improved solutions (and/or concealers) for the dark circles beneath my eyes; actually for me these have not appeared with the onset of middle age – I swear I first noticed them post freshers' week when I was a tender nineteen. I have unfortunately acquired a set of jowls to rival a bulldog which don't worry me when I look in the mirror but I have been ever so slightly horrified when someone posts a photograph of me looking jowly, or on occasion when I catch a

---

[14] This doesn't just apply to beauty products. I defy anyone not to thrill at the unbridled joy of unwrapping an Apple product.

[15] Quick beauty tip: When applying mascara, use a toothpick to individually separate lashes. I once bought an implement to do this job called a Savvylash 'gives you the power to achieve lash perfection', it wasn't hugely expensive, a fiver maybe, but it snapped after a short time and I realised that a plain ole plastic interdental tool would do the job just as well.

glimpse of a haggard-looking me in the mirror when in a store that has 'orrible fluorescent lighting – I'm looking at you Marks & Spencer.

So, I think it's become clear that grooming is important to your mother and while I've said that my hair is a curly mess I feel the need to impress on you the importance of a good hairdresser, one that you can come to know and love. In my opinion it is more important to invest in a good hair cut than any amount of clothes, accessories or make-up. It puzzles me why some people spend so very little time, money and effort on something that they wear every day.

Shopping in general is a passion, whether buying stuff for myself, my home or other people and it doesn't matter if I'm not the person making the purchases – as long as someone is having a retail triumph or two I am happy.

'Whoever said money can't buy happiness simply didn't know where to go shopping.' Bo Derek

I do find though that shopping with more than one other person is a pointless, frustrating exercise. To be honest I am happiest as a lone shopper and I don't necessarily have to spend a zillion pounds either to have a good day at the shops. A long leisurely browse in a bookshop is hard to beat; a madly discounted designer something or other from TK Maxx can make me grin broadly; a plain bare wood pencil or a sheet or two of smooth matt thick quality wrapping paper can do the same; or a new purse. A new purse purchase is a sublime event. I am presently on the wagon when it comes to purse procurement and have, in fact, had my current purse – a huge Orla Kiely one with an old-fashioned clasp – for years. As I write this I am fighting the urge to look online for a replacement.

I like buying shoes, of course I do. I particularly love loafers and boots. I tend to avoid anything higher than a 'mid heel' as I simply cannot walk in high heels without looking like a man in drag. Des says I remind him of Dick Emery (google him) in one of his 'Ooh you are awful…but I like you' sketches when I wear heels. Luckily I'm fairly tall for a woman, 5' 10", so I don't need the heels to elevate myself, I just love the way they make your legs look better. I do love being tall. This doesn't mean I look down on people who are short; hang on, actually it does, but you know what I mean here. I wonder how tall you would have been.

If I were to make a list of people I admire it might tell you something about me; a lot of them would be writers but the range of people is so broad and varied that a big long list would just bore you so I'll speak of the personal qualities I admire and that will show you something of my values; the qualities I hold dear, that have helped me navigate my way through my life so far. Kindness, is for me, *the* most important quality of all.

'Kindness in words creates confidence, kindness in thinking creates profoundness, kindness in giving creates love.' Lao-Tzu

I hope that I show it to others often enough. I am glad to say I have had it shown to me throughout my life in lots of ways and there is nothing to beat it. Other values I will tell you of will seem small and possibly petty but they're about me; so here we go.

Before I talk of the more trifling values let me tell you of a big one. This is anti-racism. I will sound naïve and I know it's far more complicated than this but I don't care, for I am genuinely puzzled how any sensible person, anyone with a couple of brain cells to rub together, cannot see that racism defies logic. I wouldn't presume that someone with grey/green eyes was mean, for example, or that a woman with curly hair was cheerful or that a chap with well-manicured hands had a good sense of humour. I could dribble on and on but I'm sure you can see what I'm getting at here. It doesn't make sense and when people do make judgements on others, I'm referring to negative perceptions here; it sickens me and ends up making me feel prejudiced against them for being so bloody ignorant. I am delighted to now be able to use a quote from one of the finest men that ever lived.

'I have a dream that my four little children will one day live in a nation where they will not be judged by the color of their skin, but by the content of their character.' Martin Luther King Jr.

To say this man is a hero of mine is an understatement.

Moving on from this most important value of mine, I will counter it with a less vital quality I would wish you to inherit. I have a need for order and tidiness. This is petty territory maybe, but it sure does make for a more peaceful life and I believe less energy sapping than living in chaos. As your parent this ideal of mine would no doubt have caused battles, probably resulting with me sighing heavily in burning martyr mode and tidying up after you (again) only to be berated by you when your things then become un-findable, but a 'de-clutter or die' lifestyle I would have enforced from time to time.

A word on housework seems appropriate here. I don't particularly *like* cleaning my house but I *love* a clean, tidy, sweet smelling, orderly home. I also love my home, so it seems only fitting that I should look after it. There are women who look down on others who care for their homes as if they've betrayed their feminist sisters in some way by engaging in this trivial activity. But looking after your daily surroundings, caring for your own space and making it a pleasure to inhabit is surely a worthy pursuit. I don't feel that cleaning is beneath me. I get a fine sense of satisfaction when it is done and my house is gleaming. I also take pleasure in using my own natural(ish) homemade cleaning products. I love the wholesomeness of them and the heavenly smells. I also go the homemade route as some chemical-laden commercial products have actually made me choke. Using these natural products makes the task more pleasant as does using fabulous tools like real feather dusters, dirt-grabbing e-cloths and tasteful real bristle wooden brushes – needless to say no 'orrible gaudy plastic neon-coloured tools in my housekeeping cupboard. Having said all this, please know that your mother is not a house-proud lunatic, forever plumping cushions and hoovering up lint from carpets. I am not a slave to the duster and there are times when my standards slip well below my happiness threshold. But as I am aware that I simply do not function well in a messy environment, I do the basics most weeks with an occasional blitz and it serves me well; so 'to bring order where there be chaos' calms me and gives me peace. Housework is also good exercise and a gym bunny your mother is not nor never will be so a bit of vigorous hoovering[16] and scrubbing is also doing me good.

The same can be said for a spot of mild decluttering. Tackling a kitchen drawer, my wardrobe or my (creaking under the weight) shelf of recipe books and thinning things out can be very

---

[16] Quick household tip: Sprinkle lavender oil on your hoover bag, it makes the job of vacuuming so much more pleasant, and if you're short on time, a quick hoover of the hall with a lavender-enhanced bag exudes 'the whole house is spotless' allure.

rewarding; energy giving, in fact. However, if any of you children had happened to thrive in a tumult of disarray, then I would have had to concede to our differences (eventually) and eased my discomfort by requesting that you close your bedroom doors at all times so I didn't have to see the mess therein.

I cannot be bothered with fussy eaters so any pickiness at meal times would have been frowned upon and if you'd have had a little sojourn into vegetarianism, I very much doubt that it would have led to me experimenting with meat-free recipes, especially if you were to continue wearing leather shoes and jackets. No, you would have been served just the vegetables of any meal I'd prepared with the concession of a jacket potato if the ones I'd roasted in goose fat caused offence, though I really do doubt any child of mine would be able to resist.

I would have needed you to be positive, not all of the time but most of it. Grumpy, negative, empty cup types really get up my beak (love that expression). Having said avoid the grumpies, I try not to judge someone when they are. I have spoken (regularly) of not judging folk, to try to imagine walking a step or two in other people's footwear before deciding what you think of them. I have also discovered it's a fine idea to look for the good in people too. It's tempting to join in on conversations tearing an individual to shreds, it's easy to have negative thoughts about them or their behaviour, but I find if I can just switch my focus to what I think is good in them, and yes sometimes I am scraping that barrel bottom bare in order to find anything positive, there is without exception in my experience something good in everyone. If you really can't (or won't) look for the good, then to just look away in a different direction works just as well. Certainly there is no gain in focusing on their evil ways, because I have learned that you simply see more and more of them. Look for the good for long enough and eventually you will see more of it and less of the bad and do you know what? Looking for the good in people *feels* better. In the past when I have felt a person has wounded me and I've looked for confirmation that this person is bad, it has ended up feeling like a poison inside me, festering and growing. To change focus feels like blessed relief. It takes so much less energy. To hate or resent somebody is exhausting. Letting go of those feelings and swapping them for lighter, gentler thoughts is liberating, freeing and energising.

'Resentment is like drinking poison and then hoping it will kill your enemies.' Nelson Mandela

I've mentioned kindness as my top personal quality. I also do appreciate good manners. I think politeness and general courtesies make for a more pleasurable existence. I would have forced you to hand-write thank-you notes for gifts and money. OK, when battle weary I might have conceded to allow an email or a message via Facebook to suffice but a 'thank you' you would have made and quite possibly I'd have checked the spelling on it too. I physically wince at a misspelt word. I can forgive it in the very young but it can really spoil my day otherwise. There is a delightful café local to me that has a blackboard notice stating that 'sandwichs' are available. I am itching to insert the missing 'e' every time I drive past it. Misuse of words annoys me too. 'Your welcome'; no '*your*' not actually; '*you're* welcome'.

A thank-you note can often be a chore to do for the young (and the time-pressed old for that matter) but to receive them is a joy (even one with a plethora of misspellings). The impact of a thank you from a child on folk like me is immense. I have a sheaf of the most charming thank-you notes and I treasure them. Our nephew's thank-you card when we gave him a puppy makes me smile just to think about it. It just doubles up the joy of giving for me. The absence of a show of gratitude does the opposite. I have been known to simmer with resentment towards those newly-weds who haven't had the courtesy to drop me a line after the confetti has biodegraded. I feel a rant coming on…

What is going on with people who don't say thank you for a gift? It's a simple thing, especially these days, though I obviously prefer the personal touch, but it really is so easy to print off a standard, one size fits all, thank-you note after big occasions, or small ones for that matter, but no word at all is I'm afraid unacceptable. I hear that sending thank-you cards isn't the done thing any more and that makes me sad as I don't want to imagine a world where making someone feel appreciated isn't worth doing. When I have put considerable time and thought into choosing a gift, or have written a large cheque (or even a small one), or have taken time to bake a cake, or just hung a bag of runner beans on someone's door handle, to not have it even acknowledged is (in my opinion) sheer lack of manners and just rude. My dislike of 'rude' again – another repeating theme. I don't just mean a show of appreciation for gifts (big or small) but saying thank you for good deeds would have been another essential practice of your childhood. I don't mean to be prescriptive about thank yous here, I'm certainly not suggesting a carefully selected greeting card, handwritten and sent through the post (though these are by far the very best to receive) but a simple text message (outlay of time approximately thirty seconds) or an email would do. When I have delivered a parcel of home baking to someone's doorstep to find myself wondering if the dog has eaten the contents (until the tin I left it in is returned) makes me cross or, rather, it makes me feel taken for granted.

In fact, the words 'thank you' and 'please' would have been some of the first words I would have taught you. If anyone asks me for anything without using the word please, it sounds like an unfinished sentence to me. I find myself automatically adding it when it's omitted and that doesn't just apply to children or to the word 'please'. A 'please' pretty much has to be followed by a 'thank you' in my book. These small courtesies shown to one another are very important for our well-being I think and while their use is routine (it is in my household at least) I still think it shows respect and consideration and therefore, in my view, is very important. Just saying…

Another valuable quality that I would wish you to inherit, though not from me as I am still struggling to put it into practice myself, is to have a healthy respect of self. My husband Des has it in abundance and taught me a valuable lesson in week one of our relationship. I was still in 'walking wounded' mode post my marriage breakdown and I suppose reluctant to even think about committing to anyone new. Add to that the fact that Des was truly not my type meant I was wrestling with the idea that I could ever be serious about someone like him. The first weekend we spent together I said this to him: 'I'm not sure I'm ready for a relationship with you. Perhaps we could see each other just when I visit Cornwall.' I added with a laugh: 'You can be my Cornish shag!' Ha! Good grief. What was I thinking of? I am aghast when I think of it. However, if someone I was keen on had made that announcement to me, I'm pretty certain I'd have settled for it, taking the view that I would build on it; bring the person round and win them over by making myself irresistible.

Not Des. He didn't say much at the time but later that evening he said that it wouldn't be enough for him, he had fallen for me and that if he couldn't have a relationship with me, he didn't want anything at all. Whoa. That took me aback. It showed me he wasn't prepared to settle for second best, that he had sufficient self-respect and self-worth to say: 'No, that's not enough for me, I deserve more.' He did and it made me look at him in a different light. It bloody worked too, didn't it?

So, I would have hoped to instil in you the importance of self-respect, even if I don't manage this for myself often enough. I think it's possibly because of the people-pleasing side to my nature that runs counter to it from time to time but I'm pleased to report that since entering my fifties I am gradually shedding this affliction.

'The eyes of others our prisons; their thoughts our cages.' Virginia Woolf

Another quality that I would like you to have though I'm not sure I have it myself, is to be a good listener. I'm working on it. My mother is a great listener so I hope it is a quality I would more easily have honed should I have had children. For sure I would have truly wanted to hear all about your triumphs, joys, troubles and woes. I have had the occasion to play this role a number of times to some of the young people in my life and it has always been a privilege though I suspect my tendency to finish people's sentences and even put words into their mouths might have got in the way of the listening, but not all of the time I hope.

The thing is, I am a great talker both to others and to myself. In fact, my husband often says he can't get a word in with a hammer and chisel. I talk to myself ALL the time. I'm not alone in this I know, but I'm not sure other people have quite so many imaginary conversations with other people, some invented people and some real. I talk to our dogs. I will greet them with a 'Morning ladies' before I take them for a walk and I always thank the chickens for laying me their precious eggs. I used to tell our (sadly departed) feral tomcat Smokey Joe what was on the menu. I would open the food pouch and say to him 'Chicken in Jelly today, Smokey.' Clearly I've already embraced the 'batty' bit of aunty I wanted to develop.

Barmy mothers are, I suspect, embarrassing at the time, but fun to look back on. I think also if the 'a bit mad' part is also combined with some degree of practicality then all is good and while a dreamer I also have a very practical side to my nature. I'd have put up shelves in your bedrooms, and as you know I think of myself as an accomplished decorator, so would have inflicted my tastes on your rooms for as long as I could; buying antique/vintage furniture for them and painting the walls in subtle Farrow & Ball shades. You most likely would have had to suffer a big bold French bed and as one of my passions is a fabulously dressed bed, I'd have imposed a plethora of pillows, cushions and throws to dress it with. As I know my way around a sewing machine and a needle and thread I'd have made you curtains, cushions etc. I'd have also had a crack at making the odd fancy dress costume and no doubt replaced buttons and repaired the odd torn favourite shirt. I was going to add sewn your name labels in your PE kit but I'm not sure that happens any more.

I'd have baked you cakes and tried, I suspect, far too hard to create something spectacular on your birthdays, which probably would have tasted fine but looked a little wobbly. Without doubt I would like to have made your birthdays memorable and they would have been days for major celebration. I've imagined many a traditional jelly-and-cake style occasion, with no fancy entertainers, just a bit of pass the parcel, pin the tail on the donkey and squeak piggy squeak. I'd have festooned the house with banners and greeted you from school breathless from the blowing up of balloons. I'd probably have spent far too much on special napkins and 'happy birthday' table sprinkles (which I would later curse when still finding them to hoover up weeks later).

I think it's very important to celebrate whenever we possibly can. Make a fuss, serve a feast, open a bottle of something fizzy; whatever the occasion I am keen to mark it in some way. So exams done/over with/finished would be celebrated; followed by exam results (whatever the grade); driving tests, job interviews; all of life's milestones with some trivial, silly occasions in-between. I *always* keep a bottle of champagne in the fridge ready to revel in an unexpected glory. I'd like to think I'd have had a child friendly equivalent in the building for such occasions in your childhood, a bottle of 'posh' lemonade or a pressé of some sort from Belvoir Fruit Farms on standby and chocolate cakes lying in wait in the freezer. The reality might have been different, I might have been so exhausted and depleted from the practical drudgery of doing your washing and tidying your rooms, preparing meals and juggling a career that all I could manage would be a trip to McDonald's and a cake from Tesco's but actually do you know what? That would have been just fine.

So if your early years would have been a fun-filled heaven, a potato print world of baking, story reading, trips to the beach, boating, fishing and so on, what sort of mother would I have been to you when school and career choices loomed? I'm not sure what career advice is like at schools these days, though I have asked my teacher friends and gather it is something that is often under-resourced. It was pretty rubbish at my school. I remember just the one session where I'd shared my interest in fashion. 'It's dog eat dog in the rag trade,' said the 'advisor' and dismissed the notion in a trice. There was no exploration of how the broader world of fashion might have been accessed. Fashion journalism maybe, fashion retail or event organising or as stylist or photographer, a whole plethora of careers linked to the industry that could have been looked into. But why shut the door on creative ambition? Fashion designer to the stars is not such an impossible goal; someone's got to do it.

'Keep away from people who try to belittle your ambitions. Small people always do that, but the really great make you feel that you, too, can become great.' Mark Twain

I truly agree with Mark Twain here, but I suspect if any of you had grown up to been fearless adventurers I'd have been way too frightened for you to have been of much support. I suspect if it was the heart's desire of one of you to say walk a tightrope stretched across Niagara Falls I, sadly, would not be available to cheer you on, but would be sitting by a phone in a terrified haze.

I hope that if I'd developed the 'listening' gene I would have helped you to find your passion, your life's purpose. Helped you to follow your dreams. It is hard to know what we are here for and what would give us most fulfilment. I have hinted at the spiritual side to my nature but it's a side of me I largely keep under wraps. I'm not ashamed; I'm just not the tree-hugging, purple-wearing type and though I hold with many of the so-called 'new-age' values I don't feel the need to label myself in that way. Neither do I want to preach my beliefs to others, but rather just live by them, as best I can. For sure my interest in metaphysics has helped me boost the positive disposition I was lucky to be born with and through that I've managed to turn the dark times I have been through into tools to learn from, the pearl from the grit in the oyster.

'The greater part of our happiness or misery depends upon our dispositions, and not upon our circumstances.' Martha Washington

The most important thing I have learned is that life is *meant* to be happy and if it isn't we can change it. I have one or two friends with whom I share this part of me and that is enough. I would have shared it with you too; even if it meant you thought I was a bit crazy. It's surely better than having a negative moaning old bat for a mother.

It's easy as the parent of imaginary children for me to say I would have encouraged you children to go for lives and careers that just simply made you happy however impossible your dreams might have seemed.

'Everybody is a genius. But if you judge a fish by its ability to climb a tree, it will live its whole life believing that it is stupid.' Albert Einstein

I like to think I would have very quietly guided you within the boundaries of our education system to spot what your passions were and to have encouraged you to follow them however mad or hare-brained. Though you may have inherited my 'people pleasing' gene and only voiced ambitions that you knew would suit me. Complicated isn't it? Luckily I'm not under the pressures of our society to push you to lofty academic achievements, or sporting triumphs. I don't have to mourn the lack of A*s and blame your teachers or myself. But I believe that whatever someone's wealth, intelligence or achievements are, the only really successful person is a happy one, whether living in a shoebox or a mansion. In my view any parent who has raised a child that has had a happy childhood can sigh with contentment at a job well done.

I hope that I would have encouraged independence. This would be following a pattern from my own parents, where we were always urged to be self-reliant. For me there is something very unappealing about an adult, male or female, who depends on a parent for anything. It's just not sexy.

'A slavish bondage to parents cramps every faculty of the mind.'
Mary Wollstonecraft, A Vindication of the Rights of Woman

I would have suggested that you feel your way into things. Not trying to be good and perfect, or to please others at your own expense (me?). It's never any good either to control or manipulate others for your own benefit. Mostly I think it's important to feel gratitude for what you do have, for what is going well in your lives and to take the time to express that to others.

Something else I would recommend before making any decision however big or small is to simply follow your intuition, your gut feeling, your emotions. It's ALWAYS the right way to go. Something as simple as turning right when your Sat Nav says turn left, if it feels right to go right, go right. Am I making sense? Actually lectures on navigating from me are a bit inappropriate as I am notorious for getting lost, that's because I lack the confidence to follow my gut feeling when driving I think (?). But I sincerely believe that following your natural instincts in life will rarely let you down.

Once you had decided, or at least had an idea of what you might like to do with your lives, I would have suggested that you act 'as if' you were already where you wanted to be: the film star, the footballer, the aid worker, the hairdresser, the chef, the Tax Inspector (?). This works. I have a small example in my own life to share and a bigger one in the life of someone else.

My own was during the months when Des and I were hoping to buy our dream home, the farmhouse we now live in. We hadn't even got contracts drawn up but I went ahead and had some correspondence cards printed with our name above the address of the farmhouse we wanted to buy. It wasn't a huge outlay, I didn't order a heavy-weight vellum card with gold-leaf script, but there it was, our correspondence cards with our names printed above our dream address. We were gazumped shortly after the beautifully printed cards arrived. A cash buyer with much more to spend had arrived on the scene. My cards appeared to be redundant. Doubts did crowd in at that point but I hung on to my dream and when we visited the property again to renegotiate, I just had the strongest sense of knowing that this home, despite the odds now stacking against this outcome, would be ours. I think by having the cards printed I was sending a strong message to the Universe that I expected this house to become my home. The cash buyer melted away and I am sitting at my desk looking out at the beautiful views from my farmhouse window, writing this letter to you. It is also the home that has given me the most joy and I've lived in a fair few 'dream' homes in my time.

'The thing always happens that you really believe in; and the belief in a thing makes it happen.' Frank Lloyd Wright

A small success maybe, but I've seen it in another. I mentioned that I'd studied interior design at Chelsea College of Art. There I met and became great friends with a man called Paul. I probably would have married him but unfortunately for me he was gay. He did once say that he'd have married me too, but wouldn't have been able to do the 'technical bits' – his words. Paul had (has, he's not dead) the most fantastic sense of humour and his company was a salve and tonic for me. A gay man is just the best thing for a broken-hearted, recently separated, straight woman. You get some fabulous male company without any ne-gotiating around a 'relationship' or 'just friends' scenario; no 'do we have sex as friends' crap. Paul was fun-seeking and at times outrageous; he introduced me to parts of London life I had never seen before (or since). He gave me great fashion advice; ideas on how I might change my lifestyle and my look. He also made me laugh; a lot. He was a loving friend to me during that time, as I hope I was to him. He was heaven sent.

Paul and I came together on the interior design course largely because we were both going through a sort of transition in our lives. Me from 'baby obsessive married' to 'sad single searching for redemption'. Paul was a bit vague about his time prior to the course but I gathered he'd had something of a wild time, as Paul called this period of study at Chelsea his 'rehab'. I just about scraped through the course, mostly I imagine because I'd garnered the pity vote as I was going through a divorce. Paul failed. He didn't care; his heart was never in it; and he was never going to be a failure.

Paul is now a multi-millionaire interior designer/developer to the stars. He could be self-deprecating but always had a sharp in-stinct for good design. He used to act as if he was 'someone' a lot and now he is. Sorry if that sounds counter to my happy living in a shoebox proclamation earlier but I think you know what I mean. I'll give you an example of how I believe Paul was sowing the seeds for his later success.

The occasion was the opening of a new Armani store on Bond Street. I'm not sure how, but Paul wangled an invitation to the glittering star-studded opening and he hired himself a limo to attend. He asked another girl on the course to accompany him, at the time I was slightly affronted that he didn't ask me, but the woman he chose was a rich exotic beauty with a foreign accent so with hindsight I can see why. So Paul paid for his car to roll up at the store and deliver him and his companion alongside the other celebrities arriving in sleek black limousines. At the time I thought it a bit sad that he'd felt he had to pretend he was impossibly rich and successful. Wasn't it a bit of a sham, when he was really just a student? But I now know it wasn't. Paul was arriving VIP style because that was where he knew he belonged and where he would soon be. It was a prediction of his future. A message he sent to the Universe and so it joined in and delivered him into his rightful position on this earth.

My friendship with Paul was in a particular phase of my life. It was an extremely close, quite intense friendship for a relatively short time. Its shortness does not make it any less valuable to me. The closeness fizzled out quite naturally with no ill feeling. It was a 'horses for courses' type of relationship; we were good for each other and needed each other during that transitional time. As I embraced my rural existence in Cornwall and Paul embarked on his star-studded role the connection between us quite naturally lessened.

I am also lucky enough to have had friendships that have lasted decades. Every year I meet with three girlfriends from my student days. It's not particularly significant, just a quirky fact that these three women happen to have been my bridesmaids (along with my ex sister-in-law) at my first crack at marriage. I had made my own wedding dress copied from one I'd tried on in the designer room at Liberty's. I admit the countless covered buttons and their opposing fabric hoops that formed the attractive detail down the back were the labour of my mother. She took over when 'the love in every stitch' phase had well and truly passed. While my mother patiently hand sewed the delicate finishing touches to my own gown I (with my sewing machine perched on a small stool in my tiny north London flat) made my bridesmaids' outfits. At the time I felt rather smug about them. I thought them to be 'different' and trendy. No satin puffed sleeves or sweetheart necklines for me. No, my supporting tribe were to wear straw boaters in pink, lilac, aqua and peach, with matching gathered wide skirts with an inch of white petticoats showing beneath. It was the eighties so they were accessorised with large hoop earrings and white lace fingerless gloves; they were 'Banarama Bridesmaids' and they are *still* friends with me.

'It is one of the blessings of old friends that you can afford to be stupid with them.' Ralph Waldo Emerson

There is a joy in lasting friendships where after an absence of contact, it feels like yesterday when you see one another again. We all lead quite different lives now but come together every year with a special bond, that of simply just knowing each other so very well. I think there is a special outcome from the longevity of a friendship and that is we forgive each other our foibles and just love each other anyway. When we meet we rarely reminisce on the past; we talk about our now. Over the years we have shared our individual experiences of all that life is; from careers, motherhood and non-motherhood, marriage, divorce and singledom, and presently menopause symptoms[17] and empty nests. I'm sure we'll still be meeting up, drinking too much and laughing rather too loudly in bars and restaurants when the subjects are hip replacements and nursing homes.

---

[17] Menopausal symptoms seem particularly cruel to bestow on an infertile woman for whom menstruating has served no purpose whatsoever. To then have to put up with the discomfort that goes with the cessation of periods is rubbing salt in. However, I am being spared anything too major in that department so I am supremely grateful, particularly for the recent abatement of hot flushes.

I would hope that you children would enjoy rich, close friendships in your lives, for these are the ones that matter. Having several hundred friends on Facebook is fine. A 'Like' on a status update is fun. But close friends take time, so you cannot have a lot of them. A lot of close friends is to me a contradiction in terms; those friendships must be diluted. We're talking quality not quantity here. However, once a closeness has been developed it becomes lasting and time together is not so vital. Friendships can change; sometimes a change in status can mean that things you had in common, things that cemented the friendship are no longer there. Some friends could also have become a 'drain' and you know what I've said about friends like that. I have a quote here that I'd like to share but sadly have no idea who said it but I think it's a valuable advice as to how to be around others.

'No one should feel anything but comfortable in your company.'

This may sound a little random and I wouldn't suggest you judge someone by their handshake, but do try to make your handshakes a pleasure to receive. I find a wet-fish style placing of the hand for grasping is not helpful in winning me over. It doesn't require physical strength to offer a firm, reassuring grip, so even if you end up with weedy arms from years of pen pushing, I would urge you to exert some pressure when shaking a hand.

Also I have to admit being averse to those people, who when greeting you with a kiss, spin their heads around so fast you end up kissing the back of their neck. What is that all about? Avoiding intimacy is my assumption – I'm always suspicious of that. I'll accept this behaviour from an adolescent boy but otherwise kiss me on or near the lips please, or even on the cheek, but don't turn away so fast that it appears you are disgusted by my advances; it's just a kiss. I have friends who do this so it's not a deal breaker but I don't like it. The 'double kiss' I also find faintly annoying. Yes I do them, but I feel it's rather more British to just do the one. I think it used to be thought of as up-market, upper-class sort of behaviour until Cilla Black took it up on *Blind Date*. The trouble comes when you don't know (or you've forgotten) whether someone is a double kisser or not. Pull away from a single kiss and get bashed on the nose by the person returning for their second; awkward.

Has being childless affected my friendships? I am pleased to report that I have never felt my lack of children has made any impact on my relationships with those close friends who are parents. I guess there have been things they may have chosen not to share with me because of my lack of parenting experience. I am always quick to praise the parents of children and young people who I think are doing a good job. I will tell them that I think their kids are great and that they are a credit to them and I watch them puff up with pride and it gives me enormous pleasure.

Part of being a good friend is the ability to keep a confidence. While I said earlier I am a great talker, when someone tells me something they don't want to go any further I can guarantee it won't. I have an 'off' button in my head that never fails to operate. When someone shares a confidence with me the knowledge is filed away and never shared, however much alcohol has been imbibed. I'm glad about that; it feels like a lucky quirk. I hope that you might have inherited it from me, or learned it from me. Some people have the best of intentions but they just can't keep it in, the secret just pops out. My advice to you children is this; anyone who ever says to you, 'Don't tell anyone but…' is never to be trusted with anything you don't want to go viral.

I'm particularly gratified for this confidence-keeping ability living in a small community. As we mostly know each other, it seems to follow that we also know each other's business. I think it's because I'm quite a private person that I don't like gossip particularly. Don't get me wrong I do join in from time to time – especially if it's scandalous, it's just too irresistible – but I always feel poisoned afterwards. So unless I'm simply trying to make sense of someone's behaviour I try to avoid tittle-tattle and therefore delight in the friends that I have where we rarely touch on the affairs of others (too busy talking about ourselves probably). Besides, gossip can be damaging, especially when it's exaggerated (as it almost always is), misconstrued or simply invented, as in the tabloid press coverage of celebrity antics; if it's not juicy enough, embellish, exaggerate and when lacking in facts make 'em up. Sometimes I know I'm not sufficiently assertive to say that I don't like where the conversation is going if it's getting bitchy. I just don't say very much and I don't much like myself during or after such exchanges.

'Gossip is a sort of smoke that comes from the dirty tobacco-pipes of those who diffuse it: it proves nothing but the bad taste of the smoker.'
George Eliot, Daniel Deronda

Another element of rural life I struggle with, and I think it is essentially a country living thang, is the habit of turning up unannounced at the homes of others. I'm glad to welcome people into my home and once I've got over the 'surprise' of their out-of-the blue arrival I forget myself and simply enjoy their company. It's not that I'm likely to be caught athwart the kitchen table being shagged rigid by the Under Gardener but I'd just rather they rang first to check whether it's convenient. I think it shows a lack of respect for another's time, i.e. 'They'll be happy to drop whatever it is they're doing when I pitch up on their doorstep.' Mostly I am happy to divert my attention; I'd just rather have a five-minute warning.

I have talked about the mother I think I might have been and cheerfully glossed over many of my failings, my character flaws. If you are to know me I need to tell you of them as best I can. I was going to write procrastination first, but I thought I'd wait and write of that tomorrow. Boom! Boom![18]

'I swing between procrastination and being really thorough so either way things aren't getting done quickly.' Freema Agyeman

Me too.

I'm not sure if many parents 'fess up to their flaws. I guess they wouldn't need to as they'd be fairly obvious, especially to teenage children. As a 'make-believe' mum I will. I'm pretty sure I would have apologised to you when these less than perfect parts of me spilled over and as a result I had treated you unfairly. I say sorry easily and freely. I don't think it's a sign of weakness. If you've

---

[18] Not sure if this footnote is necessary as I think 'Boom! Boom!' is in common usage, but it originated with a puppet famous in my childhood called Basil Brush – google him.

got something wrong and you know it, then bloody well say so. I apologise a lot, as so often I think I'm right and then it turns out that I was wrong after all. It's a common failing surely but it's never pleasant to be corrected, so don't expect a positive response when you assert your beliefs above others. Sometimes it's better to just think to yourself 'Do I want to be right or do I want to be happy?' – I know I've cribbed this idea from someone else but I can't remember where I read it; suffice to say my advice would be, plump for happy. We all get it wrong; overreact; fly off the handle. It's called being human. I make it a rule to apologise whenever I've been grumpy or misunderstood a situation, or placed my own agenda on to others. I have friends who aren't disposed in this way. I don't blame them; I know they feel remorse at times. I know too that they'd probably feel some relief if they just acknowledged this and proffered a branch from the olive tree of life. Apologies are for me like Band-Aid, they help the healing process; if the person who's hurt my feelings can't or won't say sorry then I apply my own sticking plaster, as festering wounds are bad news. I'm sounding like I've swallowed a self-help book here, understandable as I have digested a few but it's something I would have liked to pass on to you. I've just read that back and realise to my shame that even though I profess to be writing to you of my flaws in this section of the letter, I've already managed to put in a positive; forgive me.

Here's another flaw to counter that. I've mentioned 'burning martyr' in relation to my fertility problems and there is a thread of that running through me. I will stoically graft away at this and that, pretending all is well in my world and then I will explode in a plume of self-pity. Poor me, no one ever does anything for me. All those around me are bewildered as to where this outburst has come from. The thing is, I need praise and I overreact to criticism. That teacher was right when he said I don't take correction 'graciously' – I didn't then and I still don't. Unless the criticism is constructive and is from the voice of someone I respect and/or admire, I take it very personally. Let me give you an example: if Des tells me there is not enough saffron in my Cornish saffron buns, I will scowl at him and will silently vow never to bake them again. However, if the silver fox, Paul Hollywood, was to bite into my buns (?) fixing me a gaze with those mesmerising blue eyes and suggest more saffron, then affronted I would not be, for he is a professional baker who knows better, plus quite frankly he could knead my dough with those big strong arms of his any day of the week. I'm letting my unruly imagination scamper off here, but I think you get my gist. Worse is the criticism received from a small child; of course, I tell myself he or she is only five and a half and bite my lip. I feel faintly ridiculous to be offended, but I still am.

To be honest I don't do conflict very well at all and if someone has really made me angry or upset me I am mostly inclined to leave the building; extremely frustrating for the person left behind with no one to shout back at, but there. I wonder if you'd have walked away from me following a feisty argument, slamming doors and then, like me, sheepishly returning to the fore calm, contrite and full of remorse.

I am quick to assume rejection or at least interpret another's behaviour as a snub of some kind; very often it has become clear to me later that it was an overreaction on my part. My first memory of being spurned was at primary school. I think it was my sixth birthday party, I can't be sure but I can picture the scene vividly; that of me giving a party invitation to class hottie, Mark Brittan, only to see him placing same invitation in the school playground bin. The fact I can still see my six-year-old self, shrugging off the hurt and dismay tells you all you need to know here I think; that and the fact I can remember the boy's name.

I do believe it is worse to be ignored. To be rejected, insulted or maligned while negative does show some feeling or interest; to simply be passed over can cause all sorts of self-doubt.

Low self-worth and lack of self-respect are facets of me known only to those closest to me. I am aware of this at least, which I think is halfway to overcoming it.

It's quite possibly become clear already but I'll admit to you now, I'm not an adventurer. As I said earlier, I am a very timid travel-ler, more especially as I have got older. Simply taking a train to London will find me verging on OCD, checking my tickets, my seat number, my watch and the station platform display monitor rather too many times. However, if you'd shown a lust for fearless globetrotting I hope I would have waved you off with a cheery smile.

I've been brought up to dislike the 'blow your own trumpet' bri-gade. I learned this quite young; aged about five or six I was bridesmaid to a cousin of my mother's. I remember the outfit vividly; the dress, a pale sage green fabric with lace overlay, and a matching pillbox hat. All beautifully made by my dear mum. I also had a pair of silver 'party' shoes, which I had coveted for what seemed like for ever and had previously been denied. Suffice to say I was feeling good. I said to my mother: 'Lots of people have told me I look pretty!' I presume I must have sounded rather too far to the right of precocious, as my mother replied, through pinched lips: 'You don't say so yourself though, dear.' Zap. The flames of my bonfire certainly weren't going to get any fan-ning that day. That little girl wasn't being vain though, was she? Enjoying the attention? Yes probably and no one likes a show-off, constantly parping about their triumphs. She needed to learn the difference between being boastful and feeling confident. That little girl *knew* she looked good. What she needed to learn that day was that she did not need to seek proof via the approval of others to feel good about herself. What that little girl didn't know was that it would take her nigh on fifty years to suss this and still not fully live it even then!

I mentioned at the start of this letter that I suppose I am rather too concerned with vanity but there is a fine line between that and seeking confidence boosters and I think my need for admiration stems from that. I do struggle if anyone criticises my appearance, for I feel I'll do that for myself thank you very much; I know my imperfections. An adolescence afflicted by bad skin didn't help. However, that suffering has always made me appreciate far more the good looks of someone with acne scars. Brad Pitt and Philip Glenister to name but two. Mr Glenister may be pleasantly surprised to find his name in the same sentence as the Bradster but both have clearly suffered this blight on their adolescence and to find themselves deemed sex gods must surely feel good when they think of some brat at school who teased them because of their spots. There is an upside to having this sort of skin and that comes much later in life; I've found that while I still get the odd spot, skin on the oilier side of the street is less likely to be wrinkle prone.

'Zits are beauty marks.' Kurt Cobain

If you'd had spots as kids, then I would have made sure you had access to the best treatments going – no expense would have been spared to help you and your adolescent skins face the world.

The great thing about life is that it's never too late to change, and I am a patient person feeling older and just a little bit wiser. Wiser? I must be, but I am still easily led by trends and fashions and when forming an opinion can often be swayed to the opposing view. A flaw in my character? Maybe, it does run counter to my talk of instinct following earlier. However, seeing both points of view could also be seen as a positive thing and certainly wanting to know and understand the other side of any argument has got to be worthwhile.

One of the pros of being a non-mother is, of course, I won't be an aging mother. You haven't got to watch me decline into old age. You won't see lipstick on my teeth when I smile, or worse a bit of egg on the side of my mouth post breakfast, possibly attached to some facial hair (arrgh). You won't suffer if I become demented or smell of pee. I won't disapprove of your spouses or the way you raise your kids. You won't hear me carping about your career choices, your homes or that you don't feed your kids enough fresh vegetables. You won't have to help me negotiate my way around new technology; patiently explain how to reboot my Sky Digibox or help me track down where the hell my downloads have ended up on my iMac. I will never be a burden to you, my unborn children. Please God I don't become an albatross around the neck of anyone else.

My husband and I were recently reminded of this when a friend was moaning to us about having to go to hospital to visit an aging aunt; the aunt had no kids of her own so the 'chore' had fallen to the niece. Des and I smiled to ourselves and said, when she'd gone – yep that'll be us.

Happily my own mother, knocking on in years, is fit and well and luckily your grandma is in reality a grandma to my younger brother's two children, so my infertility hasn't rendered her grandchildless. Thank goodness. I think I am closer to her than I would have been had I had children. As I mentioned before it's simply meant having more time. My mum and I are great friends and close friends take a lot of time. Time that if I was raising a family I would not be so rich in. The same would be true, of course, if I had a demanding career, which I don't, so it's not just the childlessness providing the time, but we enjoy each other's company immensely and though we live far apart we have a wonderful relationship for which I am very grateful.

Talking of care for the elderly, I haven't mentioned my own dear dad very often in this letter; I'm not quite sure why that is for I was a real 'Daddy's girl' when I was little. Your grandad that would have been, you have never known obviously and sadly if you had existed, he wouldn't have known you for far too many of his final years. He suffered from Parkinson's disease in the twilight of his life and later died with dementia. A heart-breaking illness to witness and one I could hardly bear. Your grandad was a big, fun-loving man who gladly lived his life well. He had sparkle and charm and loved to laugh. We lost him in increments. He spent his last four years in a nursing home, and during the last six months of his life he became drastically reduced and shrunken, wearing a nappy, being fed like a baby, and with very little cognition of anything going on around him. Gladly your grandma, still felt a connection to him and as his devoted, loving wife, she visited him virtually every day until the day he died.

I didn't feel a connection for as long, most probably because my visits were too infrequent. At the start of his time in the nursing home I felt I could reach him. We would look at old photographs and would often be amazed at his ability to recall people's names and events from his past. In particular we would look at an old school photograph and be astonished at the names he could recall of the teachers and his fellow pupils. He would become quite animated and it became my favourite thing to do with him. At this time I was sure he could feel my love. I told him regularly how much I loved him and I am glad I did. I know I've said I don't do regrets but I do wish that I could have found the language to soothe him in the early stages of his dementia. He had many hallucinations and became delusional and fearful of many things: flooding, theft, strangers in the garden and so on. I tried to reassure him they weren't real and were caused by the side-effects of his Parkinson's drugs (which, in fact, we did blame it on initially before he was diagnosed with Lewy Body Dementia) but when on one occasion he did say to me he thought he had dementia (though he couldn't actually find the word) I again blamed the drugs when I feel I could have served him better if I'd simply asked him how he felt about that. As the disease inevitably progressed, his caring needs increased and at about the time when your grandma was becoming exhausted and overwhelmed with looking after him he was hospitalised for a short while following a fall and during this time his consultant decided that he could no longer be cared for at home and therefore a place had to be found for him in a nursing home. This was devastating news for your grandma but a relief to my brothers and me, as the toll on her well-being was becoming unsustainable.

When he was in the nursing home for much of his time there I would come away from visits feeling distressed, hopeless and helpless. I think at times I tried too hard to reach him, to find in him a sign of recognition. I struggled, perpetually to garner responses from him when I think it would have been better to simply focus on showing him my love. Instead I tried to gain confirmation that he had received it. Every time I told him I loved him I looked for a response, a hint of a smile, anything. I don't need to tell you how hard and upsetting it was to look at his glazed expressionless face and see the kind loving eyes of my father just staring at me vacantly, in a blank haze. I am also very glad that you never had to see your grandad so diminished.

The only positive I can gather from this experience is my huge admiration for the kind, dedicated care he received from the nursing staff. Dementia nurses and carers are saints. They should be exulted in our society, their status should be sky high but they are criminally undervalued and underpaid.

'Geriatric nurses! Actual angels, walking among us.' India Knight, In Your Prime

I said to them as often as I could how much we appreciated their dedication, their kindness and understanding. With them in attendance we were able just to love him, which was all we had left to do.

It seems to be a recurring theme in my life of living with a form of grief that is not 'proper' grief. Losing someone to dementia is what I call a 'living grief' in that you lose the person you love in stages. It's another mourning without definition; without due process. I 'lost' Dom and grieved for him without a ceremony or a proper goodbye. I have grieved for the loss of you without honouring how bereft it has made me feel. It seems I've been destined to do grief in a secret hidden way. I'm not saying I'm up for some brutal real grief; the fact I've just written 'real' already diminishes how it has been for me. There was no actual death in these three examples but it feels like there was. I recall that when I was seeing my marriage guidance counsellor Annie I told her that before Dom left I'd feared terribly the death of my parents, but the 'loss' of him had made me realise that I could and would survive losing a loved one. A gift he gave me in a way.

It's all got a bit heavy, hasn't it? My life isn't. I have a happy life and on the occasions when it isn't, I daydream myself a happier one. I said at the start of this letter that I don't imagine you any more, but at times I still grieve for the loss of you. It's like bereavement, you adapt, and with time it becomes less raw, but there are moments when the grief revisits me and it strikes like a hammer blow.

I recommend daydreaming. Nothing is more important than feeling good even when you have to use your imagination to feel that way.

I've saved the best quote 'til last.

'Imagination isn't merely a surplus mental department meant for entertainment, but the most essential piece of machinery we have if we are to live the lives of human beings.' Ted Hughes

I know when I sign off and 'send' this letter there will be many things I will have forgotten to tell you and many new things I will learn that I will want to pass on. I expect I will also wish I'd put something differently or perhaps not told you at all. That's OK. That's the life of any real parent.

So my angels I think I'm done. I have enjoyed writing to you, talking to you and imagining your responses to all my warblings and witterings. Know that I love you, and that I always will, so very much.

All my love,
Mum
xx

Dear Reader,

I've never really imagined you until now. You may recall my saying in the letter that I am actually a very private person and here I am putting some of my innermost thoughts out into the public domain. So why this dichotomy, why this contradiction in my personality? I simply want to share how it feels, to try to find the language to express how it is to be a childless woman in a world where women seem to be defined by their fertility.

So, who are you? Are you like me? Do you know someone like me? Are you perhaps still 'trying' and fearful of ending up childless like me? If you are fearful I hope that some of my words might have softened that for you, taken the edge off; however, I'm not sure what level of comfort they'd have given me back then.

Are you a concerned relative, friend or colleague of someone going through fertility treatment? Perhaps you are trying to understand how they feel. Well, if you are, you are already a fabulous, empathic person doing a wonderful thing and hopefully some of my musings will give you the insight you are searching for.

Are you a man trying to understand what's going on with your wife or partner? Again top person for empathy. Perhaps you are a man bereft that he hasn't got children and unable to ever say it out loud.

What can I say to you all? Just be kind. Be kind to yourselves, be kind to each other and as often as you possibly can.

Perhaps you are someone like me happily landed in the peaceful haven of acceptance. We are shaped by our experience and like many who have had a rough, painful time and caught the curved ball, we come out the other side finding ourselves enriched and to have gained a more positive outlook on life. Of course, I am not glad that I wasn't able to have children, but I am glad that I have been able to deal with it in the way that I have. But I have, at times, felt misunderstood, have you? Have you felt that you stand apart from other women? And, are you also like me, at times quietly feeling less of a woman?

Do you know, this has just got to stop. Childless women are not less than, we are not odd, we are not freaks, we are not less or better able to do our jobs, we are not selfish, we are no less loving or nurturing, and I think it's important to say we are no less maternal. We need to say this out loud.

With thanks,
Tessa Broad

'To send a letter is a good way to go somewhere without moving anything but your heart.' Phyllis Theroux

About the Author

Tessa Broad was born in Suffolk, spent her early career in London working in marketing and event management for a number of different publishers and a children's charity. She now lives in deepest rural Cornwall in an old farmhouse with her second husband and their beloved cocker spaniel. She loves gardening, football and baking and has a passion for fashion and interior design. Tessa would also love to be able to play boogie-woogie piano and is presently writing a novel about a music teacher called Penny who can.

www.tessabroad.co.uk

Sincere thanks to Mr Armar for checking the treatment details are correct and for so much more.
N A Armar, Consultant Gynaecologist, Keyhole Surgeon and Fertility Specialist, Good Health is 4 all.

www.goodhealthis4all.com

A huge thank you to the RedDoor team for their unstinting support, passion and enthusiasm; and for making this dream come true.